Information Literacy and Technology Research Projects

INFORMATION LITERACY AND TECHNOLOGY RESEARCH PROJECTS

Grades 6–9

▶▶◁ *Norma Heller*

2001
LIBRARIES UNLIMITED, INC.
and Its Division
Teacher Ideas Press
Englewood, Colorado

Libraries Unlimited, Inc.
and Its Division
Teacher Ideas Press
P.O. Box 6633
Englewood, CO 80155-6633
1-800-237-6124
www.lu.com

Library of Congress Cataloging-in-Publication Data

Heller, Norma.
    Information literacy and technology research projects : grades 6-9 / Norma Heller.
        p. cm.
    Includes bibliographical references and index.
    ISBN 1-56308-752-9 (softbound)
    1. Library orientation for middle school students--United States. 2. Information
retrieval--Study and teaching (Middle school)--United States. 3. Critical thinking--Study
and teaching (Middle school)--United States. 4. Library research--United
States--Problems, exercises, etc. 5. Information retrieval--United States--Problems,
exercises, etc. 6. Critical thinking--United States--Problems, exercises, etc. I. Title.

Z711.2 .H535 2001
027.62'6—dc21   00-059342

To Samantha with Love

Here's to success and happiness now and forever

▶▶◀ *Contents*

▶▶◀ Introduction

In 1994, when *Projects for New Technologies in Education* was published, the use of the Internet for education was in its infancy. In the few years since then it has become an everyday source of information for schools and libraries. With the use of the Internet becoming more routine and with the new emphasis on testing and assessment, the time that teachers and librarians have for planning lessons and projects is even more limited than in the past.

Information literacy involves organizing, analyzing, interpreting, and evaluating information from a variety of sources, teaching students how to be independent, self-directed learners. The focus of this book is on long-term projects using the precepts of information literacy that integrate the information gathered during research into meaningful and exciting culminating products or presentations. In **Chapter Five,** career handbooks are developed by each group that can be used for "Career Day," and in **Chapter One,** "Propaganda," a video is created using the propaganda techniques studied.

A problem or an issue to be researched that integrates many curriculum areas is presented in all the chapters. Students are part of a group that develops questions to help focus on the problem, brainstorms to devise strategies for finding information, and considers possible resources. The activities apply various skills to the issue under study. For example, **Chapter Two,** "All the Ships at Sea," teaches descriptive writing as students create logs of their journeys. Developing communication skills through oral language and writing is stressed in every chapter. Peer assessment is emphasized as students critique each others' writing, helping them understand how their own writing can be improved.

An assessment checklist that can be used for each student is included with the procedures to enable teachers to discuss with the student any problems that may occur as each activity is completed before the student goes on to the next one. Assessment is ongoing and frequent, making certain that students understand what is expected of them, keeping them on task, and adjusting their strategies when and if necessary. It is a tool to help keep track of individual student progress, a formidable task during long-term, multi-activity projects. The teacher is able to see where additional information is needed, point out possible resources, and then observe the work to make sure the student is completing the tasks correctly. A final checklist is also provided for use at the completion of the project.

Each chapter calls for the use of individual notebooks or journals, with students entering information into separate categories as a means for developing organizational skills. It's also helpful to require each group to provide a weekly progress report that includes an evaluation of the resources that were used and summaries of the work completed that week.

Criteria for grades are presented with the first activity so that the students are made aware of how they will be graded and what is expected of them. No numerical value was given for each task because you'll want to determine this for yourself depending on which parts of the project you include and the ability of your students. It might be a good idea to post these criteria on the chalkboard. During each project students work in small groups with a group goal, but individual assignments are provided and individual grades given, ensuring individual responsibility as well.

The school library media program should be integrated into the school's curriculum to help teachers help students develop skills of locating, analyzing, organizing, and evaluating information. Library skills such as learning the use of the card catalog or encyclopedia, the difference between fiction and nonfiction, and the Dewey Decimal System were once emphasized in school libraries, and traditionally taught in isolation in regularly scheduled library periods. Although many of these skills are still necessary and important, how to find information is no longer as important as using the information. Technology and the emphasis on information literacy are now changing the focus of the library program.

Technology enables students to save their productions on video- and audiotapes, use computers to enhance their writing, or produce a database using the information gathered during research. These presentations can then be shown to faculty, other classes, or community groups, and they provide students with the understanding that the information will be used productively, not just in a report to be used for a grade. For example, the art production in **Chapter Seven,** "Art and the Environment," integrates both art and the environment in a work of art that can be used to publicize a community problem and help the community find solutions to it.

Teachers and librarians know which publishers and authors are reliable and have always evaluated print material before making purchases. However, anyone with an ax to grind can do so on the Internet and sound like an expert. At the same time, the Internet is increasingly becoming the information reference of choice. It allows students to access a vast amount of information from around the world, finding current sources that may not be available in print reference material as well as expert advice from people who are there to help with student questions.

Students can easily get sidetracked with the wealth of information they are able to access and often need guidance to appropriate sites. Each chapter provides tested sites for finding information about the issue at hand.

If you want to give your students the opportunity to do some searching for themselves, **Chapter Two** provides instructions for students who haven't had much experience on the Web. **Chapter One** and **Chapter Two** include activities that focus on evaluating the Web.

Today's student lives and learns in a world that is drastically changing. This book provides support for teachers and librarians to help students think critically about using and evaluating the vast amounts of information available to them for solving real-life problems, abilities and knowledge that will be vital for living productively in the twenty-first century.

The Web sites listed here were accessed in October 2000. The addresses were correct at that time, but the Internet is a volatile medium, and URLs often change or disappear altogether. If you find you are unable to find a URL listed here, try shortening it to just after the ".edu," ".org," or ".com" to locate the home page of the author/organization; it may be possible to locate the specific site using links from the main page.

Chapter One

PROPAGANDA

Propaganda is opinion expressed for the purpose of influencing others to perform a specific action. It often uses distortion and appeals to emotions or prejudice. The use of propaganda techniques has grown in recent years, and we are all exposed to a vast number of images and opinions from the media. To become media literate, students need to understand the techniques of propaganda commonly used and be able to evaluate these messages applying critical thinking skills, and they must develop the ability to raise questions about what they read, see, and hear. The more aware youngsters are of the techniques used by the media, the more alert they become about accepting or rejecting media messages.

The purpose of this chapter is for students to learn to identify and analyze the goals and impact on the audience of different kinds of propaganda. One of the best ways for students to understand media messages is to give them the experience of developing them. Students will use print resources and the Internet to research an issue of local or national importance. They will evaluate, compare, and summarize the information they find and create a video production that uses propaganda techniques to influence their audience about the issue they have researched.

By producing videos that use propaganda techniques, students learn how to evaluate all media more critically. Video production is highly motivational because kids love to work in creative ways with technology, and it encourages cooperation and understanding as each member of the class becomes part of the production. There will be writers, actors, a director, a camera person; everyone will take part, with each student responsible for overseeing an area of the production. Video production requires extensive planning, but although it takes lots of work and lots of time, it is very satisfying for all participants.

PROCEDURE

Materials

Magazines and newspapers, student notebooks, blank videotapes, music tapes, CDs, poster board, magic markers, desktop publishing or word processing software

Equipment

Computer with Internet access, camcorder, VCR, TV set, editing equipment if available

Curriculum Connections

Social studies, language arts, media studies, technology

Objectives

Students will:

▶ locate information about an issue of local or national importance.

▶ recognize how propaganda is used to further a cause.

▶ compare print and nonprint resources.

▶ recognize the impact of media on audiences.

▶ compare and contrast propaganda techniques found in print, on the Internet, and on television.

▶ evaluate Web sites with information about the issue being researched.

▶ analyze the objectivity and credibility of Web sites.

▶ analyze the goals and effects of different types of propaganda on the intended audience.

▶ write scripts for a video production using gathered research and propaganda.

▶ learn techniques to persuade the audience to vote for their candidate.

Preparation

The research will involve an issue or cause that each group selects to see how the media use propaganda to influence public opinion. Students will evaluate print and nonprint resources, compare them, and summarize the information gathered to use for a video production.

Brainstorm with the class, define propaganda, and find examples in magazines and newspapers to familiarize students with the topic and to use for a bulletin board display. Analyze the examples, examining what each wants the reader to believe, its purpose, and what opposing points of view might be.

Brainstorm and discuss some of the ways in which the media attempt to influence the public, and have students tell about some things that they have seen or read that they believe were propaganda and if they helped change their minds or influenced them in any way. Do they believe that propaganda is always bad? Are anti-drug messages propaganda?

Activities

Activity One

The class should brainstorm for issues or causes to research and form groups based on their interests. Make sure that they get your approval before research begins. If more than one group researches the same controversial issue, each of these groups can take a different side during taping, adding interest to the final tapes.

Activity Two

This activity introduces examples of propaganda techniques. Students will find additional examples in the print media. The activity sheet and the answers to the questions, along with any examples found, should be stapled into the proper place in their notebooks.

Activity Three

Each group will find an organization involved in the issue, preferably one located in the community, and get that group's slant on it. They will also research print sources to gather information and compare and analyze the propaganda methods used by each source.

Activity Four

A Web evaluation form is included, and a separate copy of the activity sheet should be used for each Web page accessed. If the size of the group is too unwieldy, you may want students to work in pairs when they access the sites. However, each student should complete individual written assignments. You may want students to do their own searches rather than give each group suggested sites. Before students access any Web sites they find themselves, be sure to check the sites and links to ensure that they are appropriate.

Activity Five

Videotaping with an entire class and meager equipment is a labor of love. The librarian, the teacher, and any technical people willing to help should collaborate on this project. If possible, individual groups of students should work on different parts of the production. For example, while the writers are putting the finishing touches on the script the camera people can be learning their craft.

You'll need a TV set and VCR on which to watch the videos before filming is complete. You can edit using two VCRs or a VCR and your camcorder, but editing equipment makes things a lot easier. The dubbing feature on your camera can be used to add music and voice-overs. However, don't expect perfection. The process is more important than the product. If the equipment is unfamiliar to you, practice using it yourself before the students do. This project uses an individual videotape for each group because it's easier to do it that way. If you prefer you can of course use just one tape for the entire production. Have the students record each part as it is finished, then do it over until they get it right. When they begin complaining about boredom, you know it's time to stop. Many cameras have built-in titling capabilities. If this isn't available students can film titles and credits using poster board.

ASSESSMENT CHECKLIST

Student's Name _____ Class _____ Date _____

Activity Sheet 1-1   Date Checked _____

▸ Did the student:

✓ fully understand the assignment? YES__ NO __

✓ participate with the group to develop appropriate research questions? YES __ NO __

✓ begin to find print resources? YES __ NO __

✓ have a notebook prepared and divided into sections for each media type? YES __ NO __

▸ Did the group:

✓ begin to list possible controversial issues or causes and community organizations to research? YES __ NO __

▸ The student is permitted to go on to Activity 1-2. YES __ NO __

▸ If the student is not permitted to continue, note the areas of concern and further work that needs to be done.

_____

_____

_____

Activity Sheet 1-2   Date Checked _____

▸ Did the student:

✓ find examples of propaganda techniques in print media? YES __ NO __

✓ answer all the questions completely in a way that indicates understanding of the propaganda techniques listed? YES __ NO __

✓ staple all the examples in the proper place in the notebook along with the activity sheet? YES __ NO __

✓ underline the objectionable words and find suitable substitutes for them? YES __ NO __

▸ The student is permitted to go on to Activity 1-3. YES __ NO __

▸ If the student is not permitted to continue, note the areas of concern and further work that needs to be done.

_____

_____

_____

Activity Sheet 1-3   Date Checked _____

➤ Did the group:

✓ brainstorm to find an issue for research? YES __ NO __

✓ locate an organization that could provide the information about the issue they are researching? YES __ NO __

➤ Did the student:

✓ write a summary of the facts and propaganda techniques used by the organization? YES __ NO __

✓ list books that provide background information about the issue properly in the bibliography? YES __ NO __

✓ find a sufficient number of newspaper and magazine resources and properly evaluate them? YES __ NO __

✓ write a report that includes both facts and propaganda techniques, with citations indicating where they were found? YES __ NO __

✓ follow instructions and use a separate activity sheet for each Web site accessed? YES __ NO __

✓ write a summary of the facts about the issue, using who, what, where, and when? YES __ NO __

✓ compare the resources in a way that indicated that he or she used critical thinking skills in evaluating them? YES __ NO __

✓ participate in the group discussion and contribute to it? YES __ NO __

➤ The student is permitted to go on to Activity 1-4. YES __ NO __

➤ If the student is not permitted to continue, note the areas of concern and further work that needs to be done.

_____

_____

_____

Activity Sheet 1-4   Date Checked _____

➤ Did the student :

✓ access three Web sites? YES __ NO __

✓ answer all the Web evaluation questions completely and critically, indicating understanding of the subject? YES __ NO __

✓ compare all the Web sites and include all the essential points needed for a complete evaluation? YES __ NO __

Activity Sheet 1-5   Date Checked _____

➤ Did the student:

✓ watch enough TV commercials to be able to complete the questions? YES __ NO __

✓ write a report that includes a sufficient number of examples and evidence showing an understanding of the use of propaganda in all media? YES __ NO __

✓ contribute to the writing of the video scripts? YES __ NO __

✓ fulfill the task assigned to him or her? YES __ NO __

✓ contribute to the evaluation of the tape and answer all the questions? YES __ NO __

✓ participate in the class evaluation of the tapes and offer constructive criticism for improvement? YES __ NO __

▸ Did the group:

✓ make sure that each student had a double-spaced copy of the script that included the use of music and props? YES __ NO __

✓ use propaganda techniques, both pro and con, that were effectively presented? YES __ NO __

✓ correct any noticeable problems? YES __ NO __

Final Assessment   Date_____

▸ Did the student:

✓ contribute meaningful suggestions to class and group discussions? YES __ NO __

✓ keep a notebook that is well organized by media type? YES __ NO __

✓ include all the written reports, a bibliography of many varied sources, and all the activity sheets, with completed answers, in his or her notebook? YES __ NO __

✓ participate in the production of the videotape and completion of all assigned tasks? YES __ NO __

✓ complete all the required written reports, indicating a critical understanding of the propaganda techniques used by the media to influence public opinion? YES __ NO __

- Activity Sheet 1-3: A report giving all the facts found about the subject, comparing and evaluating print sources, and about the community organization, including any propaganda techniques used in any of the resources.

- Activity Sheet 1-4: A report that includes a review of each Web site accessed, using the evaluation criteria, including information received from e-mail messages; a comparison of each of the Web sites with the print resources and community organization as to accuracy and propaganda (The student should include which he or she feels is the most reliable and explain why.); and a summary of the facts found about the issue.

- Activity Sheet 1-5: A report that explains where propaganda is most effective—on TV, in print, or on the Web—with examples and evidence for opinions.

FINAL GRADE _____

NOTES _____

_____

ACTIVITY SHEET 1-1
PLANNING YOUR RESEARCH

You've been discussing propaganda in class and looking at examples of how it is used in the media. You understand what propaganda is and how it may distort information and appeal to emotions and prejudice.

Understanding the Assignment

Each student will use newspaper and magazine articles, editorials, and cartoons and analyze them for propaganda techniques.

After class discussion of local and national issues, students will form groups based on the issue they want to research.

Using community, print sources, and the Internet, the group will find information about the issue that was selected and evaluate any propaganda techniques that are used in connection with this issue.

Each group will produce a videotape that includes a speech and television advertising for a candidate who is running on a platform that includes this issue.

Each student will keep a notebook divided by media type and keep in it the copies of activity sheets, research notes, written assignments, and a bibliography.

What Information Do You Need?

What are the facts concerning the issue your group is researching?

What makes this a controversial issue?

What do the different sides concerned with the issue believe should happen?

Do they distort the facts to make you believe that their side is right?

How do they do this? Brainstorm with your group and add any additional questions you believe are necessary.

Where Will You Find the Information?

▶ **Library media center.** Books that can provide you with background material about the issue your group is researching.

▶ **Newspapers, magazines, and television.**

▶ **Community organizations involved in this issue or cause.**

How Your Grade Will Be Determined

▶ Participation and meaningful contributions to all classroom and group discussions.

▶ A well-organized notebook, divided by media type, that includes all the written reports, activity sheets, a bibliography, and indication of your having used a sufficient number of varied resources to gain an understanding of the facts concerning the issue.

▶ Participation in the production of the videotape and completion of all assigned tasks.

▶ Completion of all the following written assignments:

Activity Sheet 1-3: A report giving all the facts you found about the subject, comparing and evaluating print sources and the community organization. Include any propaganda techniques used in any of the resources.

Activity Sheet 1-4: A report that includes a review of each Web site you accessed, using the evaluation criteria. Include information you received from e-mail messages; a comparison of each of the Web sites with the print resources and the community organization as to accuracy and propaganda; and a summary of the facts you found about the issue you're researching.

Activity Sheet 1-5: A report that explains where propaganda is most effective: on TV, in print, or on the Web. Give examples and evidence for your opinion.

▶▶| ▬▬▬▬▬▬▬▬▬▬

ACTIVITY SHEET 1-2
PROPAGANDA TECHNIQUES

In class you've started discussing the propaganda techniques commonly used to influence audiences. What follows are the most common propaganda techniques and examples of each.

Look in newspapers and magazines to find additional examples. Underline the techniques you find in each newspaper or magazine article, editorial, or cartoon, and put it into your notebook, along with the answers to the questions on this activity sheet.

Vocabulary

  ▶▶ objective

  ▶▶ qualified

  ▶▶ shady

Propaganda Techniques

Bandwagon tries to persuade people to do something by telling them that others are doing it; everyone supports this candidate or cause, and therefore so should you.

> **Example:** Everyone in this town is voting for John Doe for mayor. Shouldn't you be part of this winning team?

Testimonials use the words of a famous person to persuade you. There is nothing wrong with citing a qualified source, but the testimonial is often used in ways that are deceptive. An appeal to authority is improper if the person is not qualified to have an expert opinion on the subject.

> **Example:** Athletes are often paid millions of dollars to promote sports shoes, equipment, and fast food. A movie or TV star or an athlete can interest people in an issue or a candidate and try to influence them to become supporters.

Plain folks identifies the candidate or cause with ordinary people to try convince the audience that the candidate is just like you and me and can relate to issues we care about.

> **Example:** The candidate understands our problems, even though we all know he's a millionaire living in a mansion.

Transfer uses the names or pictures of famous people, symbols, or quotes to send a message not necessarily associated with them, trying to persuade us through the use of something we respect, such as a patriotic or religious image, to promote the issue or candidate.

> **Example:** A television ad with an actor playing a "doctor" in a white coat explaining why you should use the advertised product.

Fear uses something to frighten us and tell us what we can do to avoid the terrible thing from happening.

Example: If the opposition is elected, taxes will be raised and you might lose your home.

Name-calling ties a person or cause to a negative symbol, hoping that the audience will reject the person or the idea.

Example: John Doe has communist leanings.

Staple this activity sheet and the answers to these questions in the proper place in your notebook.

- Bandwagon

    Did the use of the bandwagon make you feel that you didn't know something that was common knowledge? Explain.

    _____

- Testimonials

    Who or what is quoted in the testimonial in the piece you found?

    _____

    Without the testimonial, is this a cause that you would support?

    _____

- Plain folks

    What issue was being promoted with the use of this technique?

    _____

- Transfer

    What examples of transfer using symbols were you able to find in the newspapers and magazines?

    _____

    What issue was being promoted?

    _____

    How was the symbol meant to influence the reader?

    _____

- Fear

    Is the fear in the piece you found exaggerated to obtain the support of the reader in this piece?

    _____

    How valid is the fear?

    _____

- Name-calling

    What emotional words were used in the piece to make you feel strongly about someone or something?

    _____

In the examples you found, who used these techniques, and why?

Are these techniques always bad?

In which situations would they not be bad?

Does the cause mentioned in the article have any value?

Is the person or organization cited in the article an expert? Explain.

Is the author of the article an expert in the field?

What is it the article wants us to believe?

Do any of the examples provide useful information?

Is propaganda necessary?

Was your opinion changed after reading the article?

Which techniques in the articles you read seem the most effective?

What are some ways that readers can deal with propaganda effectively?

Underline the words that you would eliminate to offer a more objective view. What words could be substituted for them?

ACTIVITY SHEET 1-3
EVALUATING PRINT RESOURCES

All resources that you use for research need to be evaluated, whether they are print, those found on the Internet, or from an individual in a community organization. However, it's usually easier to evaluate a print source or information from a community organization than anything you may find on the Web. When you use print resources they have usually been evaluated either by an editor or fact checker, and organizations that have a particular slant are eager to enlist your help in their cause.

Vocabulary

- unbiased
- impartial
- brochure
- skeptical motive
- bogus
- motive

Your notebook should be divided into categories by media type: television, radio, magazines and newspapers, books, and the Internet. List the facts you find about the issue in your notebook in each media type, using who, what, where, when, and why. Use a separate copy of this activity sheet for each resource you use. Be sure to list all the bibliographic data your teacher wants you to include.

What is the issue or cause your group is researching?

Community Organization

Answer each question in your notebook:

▶ Name of the organization that provided you with information.

What is the purpose of this organization?

Did you get the information from an individual?

Is this person an authority on the subject? How do you know that?

Did you get information from a brochure?

Were any authorities on the subject quoted in the brochure?

How has your opinion been affected by this information?

List any propaganda techniques that were used to try to influence you.

List any new information you found out about the subject.

Write a summary giving all the facts you found about the subject and any propaganda techniques that were used to try to influence you.

Research Using Print Resources

When something is printed in a book, newspaper, or magazine there is an editor or fact checker who determines the accuracy of the information.

▶ Newspaper or magazine title: _____

▶ Date: _____

▶ Was this an article, editorial, cartoon, op-ed piece, or advertisement?

_____

▶ Who wrote the piece? _____

Books will provide background information about the issue.

▶ Title of book: _____

▶ Date of publication: _____

▶ Author or editor: _____

Comparison and Evaluation

Using each of your resources, answer the following questions in your notebook:

▸ Is the information about the issue current enough to use for your research?

▸ Are any authorities cited in the article?

▸ Is the person who wrote the piece an authority on the subject?

▸ How do you know that?

▸ Does this article use any propaganda techniques in its presentation?

▸ What new information did you learn about the issue?

▸ Has your opinion been affected by this information?

Write a report giving all the facts you found about the subject, comparing and evaluating any propaganda techniques used in any of the resources and telling where they were found and who wrote them.

Enter all the resources you used in your bibliography.

ACTIVITY SHEET 1-4
EVALUATING THE WORLD WIDE WEB

The Web provides information from all over the world, but because that information can be written by anyone with a computer and Internet access, the information offered can range from excellent to bogus and can have been supplied by people who may have a great deal of knowledge, or questionable qualifications, or an ax to grind. When looking for information on the Web, it's important to remember that the Internet is the perfect place for people to get their views across and possibly use some of the propaganda techniques you have been studying. When you access a Web site it's important to know if the site provides information that is accurate. Trying to separate fact from opinion on the Web can be difficult. Look for additional sources that agree with and confirm the information you find.

Enter your answers to the questions in this activity in your notebook, *using a separate activity sheet for each site you access.* Carefully list the name and URL of each Web site that your teacher gives you. You may need to return to the site at a later time.

Evaluating Online Resources

1. Domain Name. The suffix of a Web address can help you determine where the information is coming from. Remember these suffixes are not always accurate, but they can give a clue to the author or organization sponsoring the site.

   ✓ .com is a commercial site

   ✓ .org is usually a nonprofit organization

   ✓ .gov is a government site

   ✓ .net is a network

   ✓ .edu is an educational organization

   ✓ A tilde (~) as part of the URL is a personal page.

   ✓ Sometimes .edu sites are individual home pages of people affiliated with the institution.

   ✓ Foreign Web sites have different suffixes. For example, .ca for Canada.

   What is the URL of the site being accessed?
   Is this a commercial, governmental, organizational, personal, or educational Web site?

2. Format and Design

   Is the site difficult to read because of the way it's presented? Explain.

   Do the graphics serve any purpose other than decoration or for advertising?

   Are the graphics on the page clear and helpful or distracting and confusing?

   Was all the information you needed on the top page or easily found on another page within the site?

   Do the site's links work? Do they send you to other reliable sources of information about the topic of your research?

   What pictures, sound, movies, and other graphics are featured on this Web site?

3. Authority

    Who is the author of the Web page?

    Is the author an authority on this topic? How do you know that?

    Does the author admit that this is a controversial subject and that his or her opinion may be biased?

    Is there is an address, telephone number, and e-mail address to contact the author for further information?

    If not, can you link to a page where such information is listed? List the e-mail address:

    _____

    Using the e-mail address or telephone number, contact the author for any further information you need. List questions to ask the author in the e-mail message:

    _____

    _____

    Summarize the information you received in the reply, giving the Web page name, URL, name, author's name, and e-mail address. _____

    What do you think it may indicate if you don't get a reply?

4. Publishing organization. When evaluating information found on the Web, it's important to know who is providing the information to help you determine what their point of view or bias might be.

    Does the name of the sponsoring organization appear on the Web site?

    What is the name of the organization?

    Is this organization recognized in the field that you're researching?

    What is the author's position in the organization?

    What information about the company or organization is given on the site?

    Does the organization have an interest in the issue that might prejudice the information? Explain.

5. Date of publication

    When was the information originally published on the Web site?

    Was it published separately in print before it became available on the Web?

    What is the date of the last revision?

    Is it important for your research that the information be updated? Explain.

6. Content

    Does this site have information about the specific issue you are researching?

    Have the authors provided any supportive evidence for their conclusions?

    Are there any bibliographies, telephone numbers, or mailing addresses that can be used for further information?

    Were you able to easily read and understand the information?

Did the site add to your information or knowledge about the subject?

List any new information you gathered at this site.

What information, if any, did you gather from the links?

Circle any propaganda techniques that were used:

bandwagon	testimonial
plain folks	transfer
fear	name-calling

Explain how this technique was used.

Was the page worth visiting?

Did the information help you with your research?

Why is this information important to your research?

Will you include this site in your bibliography?

What is the purpose of this Web site?

Was the motive of this site to inform you about a topic, sell you something, or persuade you about a special interest? Explain.

Comparing Web Sites

It can be really difficult to figure out what information is accurate. One way is to compare your sources. After you access three sites to find information, list the URL and name of each site, then continue to answer the questions in your notebook.

▸ Which if any tried to persuade using propaganda techniques?

▸ Compare and contrast contradictory information among these Web sites.

▸ How will you determine which information is accurate?

▸ Write a review of each Web site you accessed using the evaluation criteria. Include any information you received from e-mail messages.

▸ Do you feel that this Web site is fair and doesn't include any propaganda? Explain.

Comparing Print Resources to the Web

Using the information above, write a report that includes:

• A review of each Web site you accessed using the evaluation criteria. Include any information you received from e-mail messages.

• A comparison of each of the Web sites to the print resources and the community organization as to accuracy and propaganda. Which do you feel is the most reliable? Why?

• A summary of the facts you found about the issue you're researching.

▶▶┥ ▬▬▬▬▬▬▬▬▬▬▬▬▬▬▬

ACTIVITY SHEET 1-5
PRODUCING A VIDEO

Your class is going to produce a video using the research you've gathered. Each group will present their view of the issue as a candidate running for office, using propaganda techniques. You'll need to write a speech for your candidate, a short advertising spot endorsing him or her, and an advertising spot discrediting the opposition.

Be sure to staple this activity sheet and the answers to all the questions in the proper place in your notebook.

Vocabulary

▶▶ credits

▶▶ discrediting

▶▶ influence

Watching TV Commercials or Political Spots

Before you begin working on your video, watch a few TV commercials in different time slots and see how advertising differs during different programs. If there is an election coming up, listen to a few political speeches and advertising spots to understand how propaganda techniques work on TV. Tape some commercials and play them a few times. Carefully watch and listen to them and write down everything you observe about the pictures, lighting, music, background, and props. Select a few of the tapes and answer these questions:

1. Time of advertising

    In what time slot was it presented?

    During what program?

    Why do you think it was shown at that time?

    What audience was this commercial trying to reach?

2. Presentation

    What kind of music was used?

    What was the purpose of the music?

    Does the music change during the commercial?

    Are there other sounds?

    How would you describe the tone of voice used by the speakers? Cheerful? Serious? Dismayed? Other?

    Why do you think this tone was used?

3. The message

Who sponsored this message?

Who would be interested in seeing it?

What propaganda techniques are used to attract the audience's attention?

Was anything left out of the message? Explain.

Do you accept or reject the message? Why?

What different reactions might other people have to it?

Write a report that explains where propaganda is most effective: on TV, in print, or on the Web. Give examples and evidence for your opinion.

Writing the Scripts

Both your candidate's speech and the commercial spot endorsing him or her will be similar because you need to make the candidate appear friendly, trustworthy, and honest in both.

1. The candidate's speech. To win an election a candidate must develop a message that is meaningful to the audience and then deliver that message effectively. The script should present the issue you are trying to get across in a dramatic way, using the propaganda techniques. Nonverbal communication such as hand gestures and facial expressions can help get your message across. Your voice can express mood and emotion. Two sentences with exactly the same words can have entirely different meanings.

2. Advertising spot endorsing your candidate. The advertising spot should be no more than one to two minutes long, but be careful to keep the most important facts that you found in your research. Political commercials express their opinion through words and music to get the audience to vote for the candidate by focusing on a specific issue, often using the propaganda techniques you've been studying. The same techniques used for the candidate's speech can be used here, but the advertising spot must be shorter.

Brainstorm with your group and answer these questions before you begin to write:

Who is the audience you are trying to reach?

What do you want them to believe?

Using both factual information and propaganda techniques, what can you write to make the audience agree with you?

Which of these propaganda techniques will accomplish this?

Select the ones you will use to help promote your candidate:

bandwagon	fear
transfer	plain folks
testimonial	name-calling

Can you think of a slogan that will help the audience support your candidate?

Sound effects can add to the impression of a candidate appearing before an enthusiastic crowd, wildly cheering. Music can enhance your candidate's position. Patriotic marches are great.

As you write your script, be sure to include what music, sounds, and props you'll need, and where they will appear.

3. Advertising spot discrediting the opposition. You need to make your opponent's ideas look threatening. Which propaganda techniques will you use to do this?

   Answer these questions before you begin to write:

      Who is the audience you are trying to reach?

      What do you want them to believe?

   Using both factual information and propaganda techniques, what can you write to make the audience agree with you?

   Which of these propaganda techniques will accomplish this? Select the ones you will use for each script:

bandwagon	fear
transfer	plain folks
testimonial	name-calling

Filming

▸▸ Brainstorm with the group to find a title for your videotape. List the possibilities here:

____

____

____

▸▸ What is the title the group decided to use?

____

1. Music and graphics. Camera close-ups of a smiling candidate convey friendliness. You may want a member of your group to play a movie star giving a testimonial. Remember, you're trying to manipulate your audience to vote for your person and mistrust the other person. Your voice and music can suggest suspicion or honesty.

   What music or other sounds will you add to make the opposition candidate appear dishonest or not deserving of the audience's vote?

   What music would make your candidate appear friendly and trustworthy? Scary music increases fear.

   What kind of graphics can you use to imply that the other candidate can't be trusted?

   Can you come up with a negative slogan for this person that uses propaganda techniques?

   How about a positive slogan for your candidate?

Music to use for your candidate _____

_____

_____

Music to use for the opposition _____

_____

_____

Will you need any props for the background? _____

_____

List all the background materials and props you need for each part of the video:

- Candidate's speech:

_____

_____

_____

- Advertising spot for your candidate:

_____

_____

_____

- Advertising spot discrediting the opposition:

_____

_____

_____

2. Credits

   Does your camera have titling capabilities?

   If not, how do you plan to show your credits?

   Will someone write them on a poster that will later be videotaped?

Tasks

When the scripts are complete, be sure that every student in the group has a double-spaced copy complete with notations for music, sounds, and any props you are using. Each member of your group will take part in the presentation. Following are some of the tasks that will be assigned to students. Your teacher will select students to fill each job.

1. Actors

   ✓ A student to take the role of the candidate. If you use a testimonial for the candidate, you'll need a student for that role.

   ✓ Someone to speak against the opposition candidate.

   ✓ Someone to do voice-overs during the advertising spot

   List the names of the students here:

   _____

   _____

   _____

2. Directors

   They will tell the actors where to stand and when to start speaking and will decide on how the props will be used.

   They will direct the camera people when to start and finish filming.

3. Artists

   They will make titles for each part of the production, if your camera can't do this.

   They will also be in charge of making the credits and making sure that everyone who helped is acknowledged.

   If any graphics are needed, the artists will make them.

4. Camera people

   They will be in charge of the filming.

5. Music director

   He or she will decide what music to use and when to use it.

   This person also will be responsible for obtaining and caring for cassette tapes or CDs.

6. Prop person

   This person will make sure that any background material used during the video is kept in good order and is available.

Evaluating Your Tape

When you finish taping, your group will review your work and see if any corrections need to be made. Don't expect everything to be perfect the first time around. You may need to do lots of editing until everyone in your group is satisfied with the results. Your teacher will give you a finishing date for when the tape must be completed.

Answer these questions and discuss them with the other members of the group:

> Are the main facts of the issues presented effectively?
>
> Were the propaganda methods effective?
>
> Did the camera zoom in or out too quickly?
>
> Is the camera zoomed in close enough?
>
> Is there anyone blocking the person speaking?
>
> Did the microphone pick up any unwanted sounds?
>
> What can we do to correct these problems?

Class Evaluation

When all the groups have completed their tapes, they will meet as a class to evaluate each other's work, using the same criteria each group used for their own work.

You should have a video showing and invite your parents, other classes, the principal, and people from the community. You might want to prepare a questionnaire to see if they can detect the propaganda techniques used.

WEB SITES

Baker, W. Frank, and Dr. N. Peter Johnson. Updated January 4, 2000. ***Media Literacy Clearinghouse***. Available: http://.129.252 .124.240:81/medialit/default.htm. (Accessed October 15, 2000).
Some of the links at this site may no longer be available, but it's worth the attempt because so much has been listed for propaganda, newspapers, magazines, and television. There is a wealth of information related to this project.

Beck, Susan. ***The Good, The Bad and The Ugly, or, Why It's a Good Idea to Evaluate Web Sources***. 1997, updated May 15, 2000. Available: http://lib.nmsu.edu/instruction /eval.html. (Accessed October 15, 2000).
Contains examples, suggestions, criteria, and bibliography. Well worth a visit.

College of Education—University of Oregon-Eugene. ***Media Literacy Online Project***. Available: http://interact.uoregon.edu /MediaLit/HomePage. (Accessed October 15, 2000).
Huge site of wonderful material divided into four sections. Be sure to access before your students do to select the proper links.

Delwiche, Aaron. ***Propaganda Table of Contents***. Updated March 12, 1995. Available: http:// carmen.artsci.washington.edu/propaganda /contents.htm. (Accessed October 15, 2000).
Although some of the material needs updating, it is still worth a visit.

Mankato Minnesota Home Page. ***Mankato MN Home Page***. © R. Bruce Farnsworth 1995–2001. Updated October 4, 2000. Available: www.lme.mankato.msus.edu/mankato /mankato.html. (Accessed October 15, 2000). Have some fun with your students and see how many errors they can find on this page. A great way to teach them not to believe everything they read! See also *Whales in the Minnesota River?*

National Archives and Records Administration. ***World War II Posters: Powers of Persuasion***. Updated August 10, 1998. Available: www.nara.gov/exhall/powers/powers .html. (Accessed October 15, 2000).
World War II posters that, although not strictly for this project, present a great overview of the use of propaganda.

New York Times Company. ***Whales in the Minnesota River?*** © 1999. Available: www.lme .mankato.msus.edu/mankato/nyt/nyt34 .html. (Accessed October 15, 2000).
Link from Mankato Minnesota Home Page. Has examples of bogus and misleading sites and how to spot them. Sure to make skeptics of your students.

PBS Online. ***The: 30 Second Candidate***. © 1998 Wisconsin Public Television. Available: www.pbs.org/30secondcandidate/text/. (Accessed October 15, 2000).
Part of PBS Democracy Project. Text version that includes a history of political commercials, the process of making television messages, and much more.

Chapter Two

ALL THE SHIPS AT SEA

We are all familiar with the wreck of the *Titanic,* the most famous shipwreck of modern times. However, not all shipwrecks are as dramatic or have been made into movies with glamorous movie stars. For hundreds of years, America was explored and settled, and its commerce conducted, almost entirely by ships. Many of these ships were lost to storms, coastlines, war, or accidents. There are hundreds of ships under the coastal waters surrounding the Americas as well as in areas of the Great Lakes, many of which have been discovered and recorded in the last few years, made possible by new technologies that have made access to them feasible. During the 1960s, as the U.S. National Park Service became aware of the importance of America's underwater cultural resources, it began to explore shipwrecks and record the findings. In 1980 the Submerged Cultural Resources Unit, staffed by professional underwater archaeologists, was formed.

Exploring the maritime history of the Americas, underwater archaeology, and shipwrecks allows for integrating geography, history, language arts, science, art, and technology into the curriculum and provides a great way for kids to use search engines to find information about a subject that smacks of adventure and excitement.

Each group of students will select a category of shipwrecks to research, including the wrecks left by pirates, commerce, slave ships, explorers, and warfare. After the resources have been searched, each student within the group will take on the role of someone involved in the shipwreck—a crew member, diver, or archaeologist—and write a log from that person's perspective, using the information gleaned from the research. After the first draft is complete students will evaluate each other's logs for accuracy, interest, and completeness, and the logs will be developed into an adventure story. The stories will then be exchanged among the groups, discussed in class, and used to write an anthology of adventure stories based on facts gathered during research.

PROCEDURE

Materials

Nonfiction and fiction books about shipwrecks; print, CD-ROM, and online encyclopedias; atlases; globes; illustrations of many kinds of diving equipment and ships from different eras; word processing software; individual journals for research and writing

Equipment

Computer with Internet access

Curriculum Connections

History, geography, language arts, art, science, technology

Objectives

Students will:

▶ select appropriate resources.

▶ decide on the kind of shipwreck to research.

▶ develop a search strategy for using search tools on the Internet.

▶ compare and contrast several search tools.

▶ compare and contrast print and Internet resources.

▶ evaluate all resources used, both print and nonprint.

▶ write a log using both objective and subjective language.

▶ participate in writing a group story.

▶ compare and contrast shipwrecks researched by the different groups.

▶ create an anthology of all the stories written by each group.

Preparation

Brainstorm with the class and have them share any knowledge they may already have about ships and underwater archaeology. Gather as many illustrations as you can find of many different types of old vessels. These can be found in magazines such as *National Geographic* or purchased from maritime museums that some of your students may have visited. Discuss whether any of the students keep a diary and the kinds of things they keep in it.

This chapter focuses on the maritime history and shipwrecks of the Americas. Suggested topics include the shipwrecks of explorers, pirates, commerce, and warfare. However, if you prefer, other regions and times can easily be substituted or added. A good start to this project might be a discussion of the *Titanic* disaster and the work of Jacques Cousteau. You might want to read *The Tempest* or *Robinson Crusoe* or stories, poems, and legends about shipwrecks with the class. There has been so much interest in recent years about the *Titanic* that this chapter does not focus on it. However, there is a plethora of excellent Web sites devoted to it, some of which are listed at the end of the chapter.

Each student will keep a journal categorizing the information found, which will be used for writing the logs. The logs will then be developed into group stories and an anthology of all the stories created.

Activity Sheets

Activity One

Before the research begins, each group should select the kind of shipwreck to research and each student must decide on the role to research: crew member, diver, or archaeologist. Several students will be crew members, and each student will decide on his or her job aboard ship. Meet with each group to be sure that all the students understand the assignment and that each student within the group is researching the topic from a different perspective.

Activity Two

This chapter assumes that students have had little experience using the Internet. The activity sheet does not cover all the intricacies of search engines. Check the results of the searches before students go on to access them, and have students access only those sites you feel are appropriate. There are four search tools listed on the activity sheet. Three are specifically geared toward youngsters; the fourth, Googles.com, is not.

After students have used the Internet search tools to find Web sites, they will go on to access the sites that you or the librarian select as appropriate. Make enough copies of this activity sheet so that each student can use a separate sheet for each accessed site. Students should print every page they access, including links that give them the information they need to complete the research. Have students use the computer in pairs but make their own notes and write their own summaries. The activity sheet provides questions for evaluation of Web sites and also questions for comparison with the encyclopedias or other books that may have been used. A list of Web addresses that are used for the project should be maintained and added to the bibliography.

Activity Three

After accessing sites with your approval, students will go on to evaluate them. To make life easier, especially if you don't have sufficient computers for an entire class to use at any one time, have the students make printouts of all the accessed Web pages and staple them into their journals. They can begin evaluations, making notes and writing summaries as other groups use the computers. Students should also be engaged in finding information from other sources, so that they will have enough resources read to complete the comparison of print and nonprint that's part of this activity sheet. A more complete Web site evaluation form is included in **Chapter One**, "Propaganda," and can be substituted depending on the ability of your students.

Activity Four

The use of the thesaurus may be old hat to your students, especially if they spend lots of time using word processing programs. The difference between objective and subjective writing may also only need to be reviewed, but for this project it's especially important for students to understand the difference when they write their logs. The class should discuss the fear of the unknown and the things that frighten them to further understand the emotions of the people starting out on a perilous journey.

Activity Five

The questions on the activity sheet will help students get started writing the log, which should of course be written in the first person. Before each log becomes part of the final story, each student in the group will partner with someone from the group for evaluation, using the guidelines on the activity sheet. The students will then put all the parts of the story together to make one grand adventure story. All the stories should be entered on the computer using whatever word processing software is available, and an anthology should be produced. Each group should be assigned to write a different part of the anthology.

▶▌ ▬▬▬▬▬▬▬▬▬▬▬▬▬▬▬▬▬▬

ASSESSMENT CHECKLIST

Student's Name _____ Class _____ Date _____

Activity Sheet 2-1   Date Checked _____

➤ Did the student:

    ✓ fully understand the assignment? YES __ NO __

    ✓ decide on the character he or she will research and join a group? YES __ NO __

    ✓ write research questions that are broad enough to find sufficient information? YES __ NO __

    ✓ begin to find and list titles and authors of print resources in a bibliography? YES __ NO __

    ✓ have a journal prepared and well-organized to begin the project? YES __ NO __

    ✓ understand the requirements for the final grade? YES __ NO __

➤ The student is permitted to go on to Activity 2-2. YES __ NO __

➤ If the student is not permitted to continue, note the areas of concern and further work that needs to be done.

_____

_____

_____

Activity Sheet 2-2   Date Checked _____

➤ Did the student:

    ✓ complete the search strategy and become ready to access the Web sites? YES __ NO __

    ✓ successfully access the search engines? YES __ NO __

    ✓ accurately list the number of hits found using each search engine? YES __ NO __

    ✓ bookmark the sites? YES __ NO __

    ✓ complete the comparison accurately? YES __ NO __

➤ The student is permitted to go on to Activity 2-3. YES __ NO __

➤ If the student is not permitted to continue, note the areas of concern and further work that needs to be done.

_____

_____

_____

Activity Sheet 2-3   Date Checked _____

➤ Did the student:

    ✓ accurately copy the URLs of the Web sites on separate activity sheets? YES __ NO __

✓ print out information relevant to the part of the research he or she is doing? YES __ NO __

✓ make accurate notes and summaries from all the relevant information and enter them in the proper category in the journal? YES __ NO __

✓ continue to list the research materials in a bibliography? YES __ NO __

✓ appropriately answer all the questions concerning evaluation, indicating a complete understanding of each part? YES __ NO __

✓ compare resources, indicating an understanding of the assignment? YES __ NO __

✓ summarize, including all the information needed to make an accurate comparison? YES __ NO __

➤ Did the group:

✓ review all the resources and review the accuracy of the bibliography, making all the necessary additions and deletions? YES __ NO __

➤ The student is permitted to go on to Activity 2-4. YES __ NO __

➤ If the student is not permitted to continue, note the areas of concern and further work that needs to be done.

_____

_____

_____

Activity Sheet 2-4   Date Checked _____

➤ Did the student:

✓ complete the exercises concerning objective and subjective writing? YES __ NO __

✓ finish the written assignments, indicating an understanding of the difference between them? YES __ NO __

✓ use the thesaurus to find descriptive words to describe the journey both objectively and subjectively? YES __ NO __

✓ write about a fearful experience and vividly describe it? YES __ NO __

✓ participate in the group discussion and offer constructive criticism? YES __ NO __

➤ The student is permitted to go on to Activity 2-5. YES __ NO __

➤ If the student is not permitted to continue, note the areas of concern and further work that needs to be done.

_____

_____

_____

Activity Sheet 2-5   Date Checked _____

➤ Did the student:

✓ understand that only the questions pertaining to the character he or she is writing about were to be answered? YES __ NO __

✓ answer enough questions to be able to make the log accurate and vivid? YES __ NO __

✓ write the log in the first person? YES __ NO __

✓ include in the log a vivid description with information from the research? YES __ NO __

✓ use information to write about how he or she felt during the trip? YES __ NO __

▸▸ Did the group:

✓ put the story together chronologically? YES __ NO __

✓ follow the guidelines for evaluation and offer constructive suggestions for improving the story? YES __ NO __

▸▸ Can the reader:

✓ derive a clear understanding of each part of the story? YES __ NO __

Final Assessment   Date _____

▸▸ Did the student:

✓ participate in all class and group discussions? YES __ NO __

✓ participate in writing and contributing ideas for the final story? YES __ NO __

✓ complete all the questions on the activity sheets, with answers entered in the proper place in the journal? YES __ NO __

✓ complete a journal that is well-organized, with a bibliography of appropriate sources, notes, summaries, and written assignments? YES __ NO __

✓ contribute to the part of the anthology assigned to the group? YES __ NO __

✓ complete all the written assignments below and indicate evidence of critical thinking? YES __ NO __

- Activity Sheet 2-3: A summary that specifies which resources were best: Internet, print, or CD-ROM encyclopedia, or a different book. The names of the best or worst Web sites that were accessed and the title of the best and worst of the encyclopedias or other books should be included.

- Activity Sheet 2-4: Objective and subjective descriptions of a good friend or pet that indicated an understanding of the difference between the two; a vividly written piece about a real-life experience that produced a fearful emotion, including a lesson learned from the experience.

- Activity Sheet 2-5: The final draft of the log, written in the first person, that included both facts learned from the research and a description of the emotions experienced on the journey. A summary of the evaluation of the partner's log, giving positive suggestions for improvement.

FINAL GRADE _____

NOTES _____

_____

ACTIVITY SHEET 2-1
PLANNING YOUR RESEARCH

We are all familiar with the wreck of the *Titanic*. However, not all shipwrecks are as dramatic or have been made into movies with glamorous movie stars. There are hundreds of ships under the coastal waters surrounding the Americas as well as in areas of the Great Lakes, many of which have been discovered and recorded in the last few years, made possible by new technology that is making these searches possible.

Shipwrecks can be caused by many different things, from hurricanes to unstable ships to bad luck or sinking by an enemy or even sabotage. For this project you will be researching the maritime history of the Americas, the shipwrecks that were frequently left in American waters, and the technology available in more recent times that makes the search for these ships possible now as never before.

Vocabulary

- ➤ archaeology
- ➤ flotilla
- ➤ artifact
- ➤ sabotage
- ➤ categories

Understanding the Assignment

After brainstorming and discussion in class, decide on the kind of shipwrecks you want to research, such as explorers, pirates, warships, or slave ships. Join a group of other students who are interested in the same topic.

Each student in the group will do research from a different point of view, and you should decide before beginning if you will be a crew member, diver, or archaeologist. Using the information you find, you'll write a log or a diary of the events from that point of view. The research done by a crew member will be very different than that of an archaeologist or diver. All the information you gather during research should be recorded in a journal kept for this assignment only.

Each group will write an adventure story based on the logs written by the students in the group. All groups will exchange their logs to compare the shipwrecks that the entire class studied. The stories will be used to create an anthology.

What Information Do You Need?

Discuss with your group the kinds of information that's needed for each student to complete the assignment, gathering all the ideas and putting them into separate categories in your journal. Using who, what, where, when, why, and how may help you decide which categories to use. Add to these categories as you do your research and eliminate others.

Develop at least three questions that will help you find your information. Some suggestions follow:

➤ What causes shipwrecks?

➤ What is the newest equipment used by divers to find hidden treasure underwater?

➤ Were there any problems associated with the ship and the voyage before the journey began?

Where Will You Find the Information?

➤ **Dictionary**. Use your dictionary or thesaurus to find as many synonyms as possible to use as keywords for your research and for descriptive language to use in your log.

➤ **Almanac**. Use the almanac or record book to find facts or statistics about shipwrecks.

➤ **Literature and music**. Can you find stories, poems, or songs written about shipwrecks?

➤ **Television**. There have been many TV broadcasts about shipwrecks and the scientists and treasure hunters who explore these ships. Be on the lookout for such documentaries.

➤ **Maritime museums**. These museums are found in many cities, and can provide you with information. How will you find the address of a museum that might have useful information? Is there one in your area? Many of these museums have Web sites.

➤ **The Internet**. Lots of the information you need is available online.

➤ **Miscellaneous**. Print, CD-ROM, online encyclopedias, and videos can give you background information about your topic.

➤ List other resources that you and the other students in your group think of.

How Your Grade Will Be Determined

➤ Meaningful participation in all class and group discussions.

➤ Participation in writing and contributing ideas for the final story.

➤ Completion of all activity sheets, with answers entered in the proper place in the journal.

➤ Keeping a complete and well-organized journal, with a bibliography, notes, summaries, and written assignments.

➤ Evidence that you contributed to the group assignment for creating the anthology.

➤ Completion of all the following required written assignments:

Activity Sheet 2-3: A summary that specifies:

- which resources were best: the Internet, the print or CD-ROM encyclopedia, or a different book.

- the names of the best or worst Web sites you accessed.

- the titles of the best and worst encyclopedias or other books

Activity Sheet 2-4:

- an objective description of a good friend or your pet.

- a subjective description of the same person or pet.

- a description of a fearful real-life experience that you had. Include what you learned about yourself from this experience.

Activity Sheet 2-5:

- The final draft of your log, written in the first person, that includes both facts learned from the research and a description of the emotions you experienced on the journey.

- An evaluation of your partner's log, giving positive suggestions for improvement.

ACTIVITY SHEET 2-2
SEARCHING THE WORLD WIDE WEB

When you go to the library to look for information you can use a catalog, or the librarian may direct you to what you need to use. If this is a library you've used before, you have a pretty good idea of where to find what you're looking for. You can head straight for your favorite author or subject, and you know that all the cookbooks or baseball books can be found in one place.

No such luck when you use the Internet. There are millions of Web pages, and the number of them keeps growing at an enormous rate. There is no catalog to direct you to the place where you can find what you're looking for. What can provide some help, however, are search tools that can guide you toward the information you want. However, using these search tools means that you must know how to ask the right questions to enable you to find what you want.

You may have used the Internet many times and have lots of experience finding information on the World Wide Web, or you may be completely new to this resource. Learning how to use search tools will prevent wasting time in fruitless searches, just as knowing how a library is organized helps you find what you are looking for quickly.

Definitions

1. The **Internet** is a huge number of computers connected together all over the world that allows users to find the latest information, ask questions of experts, and leave mail for others around the world.

2. The **World Wide Web** is part of the Internet that allows users to access text, graphics, video, and sound through the use of a *Web browser*. Every Web location has an address, or URL, which stands for *uniform* or *universal resource locator*. The URLs are sometimes very long, and when you enter them on the computer be sure to type accurately. All Web sites have a *home page,* which is similar to the table of contents in a book. This is the first page you see when you connect to the site. It has graphics, text, links to other places on the Web, and an introduction to the information found at the site. All home pages have *links* to other parts of the site and to other Web locations that give more information.

3. A **Web browser** allows you to search the Web. The Web browser you will be using is

   _____.

4. A **database** is a collection of information.

5. To **download** is to transfer computer files from one computer to another.

6. **E-mail** is a way to send messages over a computer network

7. **Boolean logic** describes a way to combine search terms. The basic operators are *and, or,* and *not.* Describe the different results your search would produce using these terms. If you are not familiar with Boolean operators, your teacher will explain them to you before you go online.

✓ shipwrecks AND pirates

✓ shipwrecks OR pirates

✓ shipwrecks NOT pirates

Many search tools allow you to find information by asking a question instead of using Boolean logic.

Search Strategy

When you look for information using the World Wide Web, you need to plan your search very carefully or you may end up with lots of useless information. Answer the following questions or do the following tasks:

1. What information are you looking for?

2. What are your research questions?

3. List your keywords or the questions you need to ask.

4. Use your dictionary or thesaurus to find synonyms or additional words with similar meaning.

5. Enter the search terms you will use.

Search Tools

Each search tool is different: Some are bigger or more current, meaning that the results of your search can be very different depending on which you use. But bigger is not necessarily better because you may end up with lots of stuff that you can't use. Examples of search tools follow:

▶ Ask Jeeves for Kids: www.ajkids.com

▶ Searchopolis: www.searchopolis.com

▶ KidsClick!: http://sunsite.berkeley.edu/KidsClick/

▶ Google: www.googles.com

Using your search terms, use the search engines selected by your teacher or librarian to conduct your search. List the names of each search tool you used, then answer the questions that follow.

▶ Search engine 1 _____

▶ Search engine 2 _____

▶ Search engine 3 _____

▶ Search engine 4 _____

How many hits did each search result in?

1. _____

2. _____

3. _____

4. _____

➥ Which was the easiest search to conduct?

➥ Did you get the same results from all of them?

➥ List the Web address(es) that you think will help you with your research.

➥ Be sure to get your teacher or librarian's approval before you access any Web sites.

Bookmarks

If you find a Web site that gives you great information and you want to go back to it at a later date, be sure to bookmark it. Your teacher or librarian will show you how to do this.

ACTIVITY SHEET 2-3
EVALUATING WEB SITES

Copy the names and the URLs of the Web sites that were approved for you to access for this project. Use a separate copy of this activity sheet for each Web site.

➤➤ Today's date: _____

➤➤ Lists of Web sites I am going to access today:

     Name: _____URL: _____

     Name: _____URL: _____

     Name: _____URL: _____

After you access the Web pages, print out every page and link you are going to use for this project. Read the printouts offline and make notes in the proper category in your journal. When your notes are complete, write a summary of the information you found. Use a *separate activity sheet* for each Web page.

     Name of site: _____URL: _____

Evaluation

When we evaluate information we get from books, we look for the authority of the author, the publisher, the copyright date, and such things as bibliographies and glossaries. The same criteria can be applied to the Web.

The following questions will help you determine how worthwhile this Web site is for this project. Enter the answers in your journal. Be sure to staple each activity sheet into your journal also.

➤➤ Is there a table of contents or a site map to help you navigate?

➤➤ Did you find the information you were looking for at this Web site?

➤➤ Did you understand the information?

➤➤ Did you find other helpful information to use?

➤➤ Did the graphics help you understand the information?

➤➤ Is there any advertising at this site?

➤➤ Did it interfere with reading or understanding the information?

➥ How do you know if the Web site you visited is maintained by someone who is an expert in the field?

➥ Enter the e-mail address found at this site: _____.

➥ Find the date this site was last updated and enter it here: _____.

➥ Is this a government, educational, or commercial site? How do you know?

➥ Are the links to another site helpful?

➥ Does the title of the page tell you what it is about?

➥ Is there an introduction on the page that tells you what is included?

➥ Does the author of the page include information that you know is wrong?

➥ If you sent an e-mail message, did you receive a prompt answer?

➥ Did the information you receive from e-mail help you?

➥ Would you recommend this site?

➥ How do you rate this site on a scale of 1 to 10, if 1 is the worst and 10 is the best?

Comparing Print, CD-ROM, and the Internet

➥ Which resource provided the best information: print or CD-ROM encyclopedia, the Internet, or a different print resource?

➥ Which was the easiest to use? Explain.

➥ Where did the best information on the Internet come from? URL: _____.

➥ In which book or encyclopedia did you find the best information?
  ✓ Title: _____
  ✓ Author: _____

➥ Was any information that you found on the Internet different from something you read about in a book? If so, how do you know which is the accurate information?

➥ Do you need to read more books, or access the Internet again?

Write a summary that specifies which resources were best: the Internet, the print or CD-ROM encyclopedia, or a different book. Include the names of the best or worst Web sites you accessed and the titles of the best and worst encyclopedias or other books.

With your group, review all the Web sites and books you used for this project, making sure that you have an accurate bibliography of all your resources. Have all the Web sites been bookmarked so that you can easily go back to them?

ACTIVITY SHEET 2-4
DESCRIPTIVE WRITING

To make this adventure story really exciting, you must use vivid language to describe how you feel at the start and during the journey. If you are a crew member, how did it feel when the ship got into trouble just before the wreck? How did it feel to see your shipmates go down? How did you survive? Or are you a diver looking for treasure or an archaeologist seeking artifacts for a museum?

Vocabulary

>> artifacts

>> convey

The Thesaurus

A thesaurus is a book of synonyms, and there are many kinds of thesauruses available. Perhaps you are using a computer program that allows you to search for synonyms online.

Objective Versus Subjective

>> *Objective descriptions* include descriptions of real things and events. Write an objective paragraph about a good friend or your pet.

>> *Subjective descriptions* tell how you feel about something or someone. Now subjectively describe the same person or animal.

When you write your log you'll use both objective and subjective descriptions.

>> The objective descriptions will include descriptions of the real people and real events involved on this trip. This is the information you got from your research.

>> The subjective descriptions will tell about how you *feel* about the trip.

Point of View

Your role as crew member, diver, or archaeologist will determine the details and features you write about. What is the point of view you are trying to convey to your audience?

Your subjective description should include details about your personal feelings. This is based on the objective, real, impersonal information you gathered during your research. For example, an objective detail is, "The girl had long red hair." A subjective description based on that detail is "Her hair was so red it looked to me like a mass of fiery snakes." Your reader should be able to close his or her eyes and actually visualize what you are describing and feeling. Don't forget to use your five senses: sight, taste, touch, hearing, and smell.

Use your thesaurus and list synonyms that you can use to describe the ship and voyage objectively, *only* from the point of view of the character you researched.

Use your thesaurus and list synonyms for the emotions you feel when embarking on this journey as a crew member, diver, or archaeologist. What are some words that you can use to describe the ship and voyage subjectively *only* for the character you researched? Remember, subjective writing tells how you feel. Would you be fearful, apprehensive, full of terror or anticipation?

Have you ever had a real-life experience that produced a similar emotion? Write a paragraph describing that experience. Have you ever been fearful of the unknown? What did you learn about yourself from this experience?

Discuss with the class the fear of the unknown. Do you think fear of the unknown ever goes away as you get older?

ACTIVITY SHEET 2-5
WRITING THE LOG

It's now time to begin writing your log. Remember, objective descriptions in the log must be based on the research you've gathered and written in chronological order with a beginning, middle, and end. But you must also include subjective descriptions that vividly explain how you feel about this journey.

This is going to be an adventure story, whether you are writing as a crew member, the captain, a diver, or an archaeologist, and must be written in the first person. It might be fun for the girls in your group who want to be crew members to act as stowaways disguised as men because there were no women working on ships at the time of the shipwrecks you studied.

After each student in your group has completed his or her log, all the logs will be evaluated by the group and put together to make one adventure story. For example, the story can begin with crew members, continue with the divers, then go on to the archaeologists who find the artifacts left behind. When an archaeologist finds an artifact it can be something that was mentioned by a crew member that got the archaeologist thinking about the person who left it behind.

Vocabulary

- ➠ applicable
- ➠ artifact
- ➠ chronological
- ➠ flotilla
- ➠ provisions

Use the answers to the following questions and the research you have in your journal to write your log. Add anything that will make the log a record of your personal experience as a crew member, diver, or archaeologist.

ANSWER ONLY THE QUESTIONS THAT APPLY TO YOUR ROLE ON THE SHIP.

Questions for Crew Members

These questions and instructions should be divided among the crew members in your group, who each have a different job on the ship.

- ➠ What kind of ship did you sail on? Explorer _____ Pirate ship _____ Warship _____ Commercial ____ Other _____

- ➠ What is the name of the ship?

- ➠ In what year did you set sail?

- ➠ Describe the type and size of the ship.

➤ What country did the ship come from? Locate your home port on a map or globe.

➤ What is its destination? In what direction will you be traveling to get there from home?

➤ When do you expect to arrive at your destination? How long is the trip expected to take?

➤ Describe the maps available at the time of your journey, if any.

➤ Compare latitude and geographic features of the destination with the latitude and geographical features of your home port.

➤ Describe the navigational equipment used on your ship

➤ What were the problems facing navigators during the time you sailed on this ship?

➤ What is the purpose of this journey?

➤ Who supplied the money for this journey?

➤ What is your name, age, and country of birth?

➤ Describe your job on the ship.

➤ Describe your daily life aboard this ship.

➤ Who are the other members of your crew?

➤ Why did you decide to take this perilous journey?

➤ What kinds of cargo did you have aboard?

➤ What were your expectations before the voyage began?

➤ How are provisions stored on the ship?

➤ What did the sailors eat and drink?

➤ If the ship must stop along the way to resupply, where does the crew plan to get supplies?

➤ What items does the crew need to survive the journey?

➤ Was the ship alone or part of a flotilla?

➤ What caused this shipwreck? Was it a storm, an enemy attack, a rough coastline, or just bad luck?

➤ Describe what happened as the ship was sinking.

➤ How did the crew try to save themselves?

‣ Explorer Ship Only:

    How did you hear about the New World?

    What was America like at the time of this shipwreck?

    Who were the people that the sailors would have encountered?

Questions for the Divers

‣ What is your name, age, and country of birth?

‣ How did you prepare for this mission?

‣ What kind of education did you need?

‣ What personality traits do you have that make you an expert diver?

‣ What kind of diving equipment are you using to find this ship?

‣ Describe the technology used to recover and explore the ship.

‣ Describe your job on the ship.

‣ Describe your daily life aboard this ship.

‣ Who are the other members of your crew?

‣ Why did you decide to take this perilous journey?

‣ Is this your first dive looking for treasure aboard a shipwreck?

‣ What is the location of the shipwreck?

‣ What was the condition of the shipwreck?

‣ Describe the type, depth, and temperature of the water in which this shipwreck was found.

‣ Where was it located?

‣ Describe the underwater features of the area in which the shipwreck took place.

‣ What are the effects of underwater currents on this rescue?

‣ What is the importance of water currents?

‣ What organisms were present in the water at the time of the dive?

‣ What kind of artifacts were you looking for?

‣ What are the laws governing shipwrecks that you must follow?

‣ What would prevent shipwrecks from happening now?

⇥ Describe how you feel before, during, and after the dive. Are you fearful or excited?

Questions for the Archaeologist

⇥ What is your name, age, and country of birth?

⇥ What organization is responsible for this mission?

⇥ What education did you need to be an underwater archaeologist?

⇥ Describe the artifacts that were found at this site.

⇥ What was their condition?

⇥ How much do you think these artifacts are worth?

⇥ What materials were they made of?

⇥ How do you know how old an artifact is?

⇥ How are the artifacts reconstructed and restored?

⇥ Who are the other members of your crew?

⇥ Describe any experience you have had as an underwater archaeologist, and any treasures you found, at another shipwreck.

Evaluating Your Partner's Log

Each student in the group will have a partner, and you will evaluate each other's logs.

This peer review means that you will read your partner's log and suggest ways that it can be improved. When you examine your partner's log, you evaluate it and make suggestions for improving it, then confer with your partner to discuss the improvements you each think should be made. Remember, the log must include both objective and subjective descriptions.

Guidelines for Evaluating

⇥ Don't evaluate based on your own style of writing or your own log.

⇥ Don't rewrite your partner's log.

⇥ Let your partner know the good things you found along with the criticisms. Evaluating doesn't mean finding only bad or incorrect stuff. Be diplomatic! Be positive!

⇥ Give concrete examples of what you think should be done to improve the log.

Does it need more details?

Should more information or descriptions be added or made more vivid?

What suggestions, if any, do you have to make the log more descriptive?

↠ Was the writer successful in adding suspenseful moments to the story?

↠ Summarize your evaluation, giving positive suggestions.

Writing the Story

After all the evaluations are complete and you have completed the final draft of your logs, you will each read it aloud to the group.

Copies of all the logs should be given to each student in the group. Brainstorm with the group for ideas for putting the logs together for the adventure story. Be sure to find a title for your story that describes it.

Comparing Shipwrecks

When all the stories are complete, they should be read aloud in class for you to discuss and compare the shipwrecks that each group researched.

Creating an Anthology

All the stories will be used to create an anthology that will be kept in the school library. Take a look at a few to get some ideas for creating yours. The anthology should include the following:

▶ A *title*, which the class should brainstorm about, that will make readers eager to read this book.

▶ An illustrated *cover* with a picture that tells what kinds of stories are included in the anthology.

▶ A *table of contents* that gives the title and page number of each story.

▶ A *title page*. What information is included on the title page?

▶ *Illustrations* that add interest to the stories.

▶ A *dedication*. Is there someone you read about to whom the class wants to dedicate the book?

▶ An *introduction*, which should include the steps that were taken during research and writing. Some interesting facts about shipwrecks should be included as well.

▶ *Biographies of the students*. These should precede each story. Each student should write his or her own biography.

▶ A *bibliography* of all the resources used by the class.

▶ *Further notes* from each group that give additional information about shipwrecks could be included.

Your teacher will assign each group a different part of the anthology to write.

WEB SITES

Corpus Christi Museum of Science and History. ***Ships of Discovery, Underwater Archaeology and Shipwrecks***. Updated September 2000. Available: www.shipsofdiscovery.org/logo.htm. (Accessed October 16, 2000).
Some harder to find information is available here: Columbus's lost ships, artifact conservation, and ships of exploration, among others.

Florida State University. ***Directory of Underwater Archaeology on the World Wide Web***. Available: http://www.adp.fsu.edu/uwdirect.html. (Accessed October 16, 2000).
This is a huge site. Scroll down all 45 pages before printing to be sure you link to something you need.

Indiana University Underwater Science Program Home Page. © 2000; updated September 21, 2000. Available: http://www.indiana.edu/ ~ scuba/. (Accessed October 16, 2000).
Many links to shipwrecks and historic sites and underwater parks, among others.

The Mariner's Museum, Newport News, VA. ***Collections and Exhibits***. © 1995, 2000; updated October 2000. Available: http://www.mariner.org/. (Accessed October 16, 2000).
Large collections with links to subjects of interest in this project.

McCraken, Peter. ***Maritime History on the Internet***. Some pages updated May 2, 2000. Available: http://ils.unc.edu/maritime/home.shtml. (Accessed October 16, 2000).
Links to museums, nautical archaeology, and music and art are useful for this project.

The National Park Service. ***Submerged Cultural Resources Unit***. Updated April 7, 1999. Available: http://www.nps.gov/scru/home.htm. (Accessed October 16, 2000).
Lots of underwater projects with information about shipwrecks listed. Also links to related sites.

Chapter Three

AMERICA AT THE TURN OF THE CENTURIES

Homelessness, racism, child labor, workers displaced by new technology, immigration, pollution. Sound familiar? These contemporary issues that are the stuff of intense debate and concern today were issues of concern at the turn of the nineteenth century as well. It was a time of extraordinary corporate growth and a rapid rise in the ranks of millionaires. The advent of big business brought immense wealth to a few people while others were living in deprivation. The growth of industry had environmental effects that have still not disappeared. Immigration was exploding, racism was rampant, women were on the march for equality. America was changing from an agrarian, self-sufficient society to one in which people became more dependent on commercially produced goods. They were times of extraordinary technological breakthroughs that brought material benefits and changes for many but hardship for others.

Many of the challenges present at that time are familiar to America at the start of the twenty-first century. Researching the similarities between the two eras makes the historical significance of those times more meaningful for students as they apply the research to issues widely discussed today. Students will research the lives of some prominent people of the era to understand their contributions to society, contributions that are still important to our lives today. Both print and online newspapers will be used to gather information about contemporary problems as well as primary source material available on the Internet to understand that present-day problems had their roots in history and did not arise from nowhere.

When all the research is complete the class will create a class newspaper with the information gathered from their research.

PROCEDURE

Materials

Nonfiction books and encyclopedias for background material; local and national newspapers; illustrations of Ellis Island, child labor, urban tenements, famous millionaires and mansions, fashions, sports and entertainers; desktop publishing or word processing software; journals for notetaking

Equipment

Computer with Internet access, scanner (if available)

Curriculum Connections

Language arts, social studies, technology

Objectives

Students will:

▶ examine the parts of newspapers and news articles.

▶ recognize the difference between local and national newspapers.

▶ compare print and online newspapers.

▶ summarize newspaper articles for information about the subject being researched.

▶ analyze editorials, cartoons, or political columns about the subject.

▶ recognize the difference between fact and opinion.

▶ read biographies of people prominent to the topic from the different eras.

▶ compare and contrast the contributions and events that led to the prominence of these people.

▶ analyze how the events and people of the late nineteenth century influenced the modern era.

▶ compare and contrast the late nineteenth century with contemporary society.

▶ write news articles about the research topic.

▶ evaluate news articles written by students to decide which should be submitted for use in the class newspaper.

▶ apply the research to the creation of a class newspaper.

▶ create a class newspaper using articles written from research material.

Preparation

Prepare a bulletin board with articles, editorials, cartoons, illustrations, and photos about contemporary issues. Explain that many of these issues are not new but rather different faces of old problems. Discuss the purpose of news and newspapers; where our news comes from; the differences in stories written by reporters, feature writers, and columnists; the various sections of the newspaper; and the differences between local and national newspapers. If possible arrange a tour of a newspaper plant or have someone from a newspaper visit the class. Discuss the changes that are taking place in the newspaper world because of the emergence of online editions.

Students will be divided into groups depending on the topic they choose to research.

Students should enter all notes and any photos, illustrations, comments, or poetry they may find about the topic in their journals. These journals should be evaluated by you as each activity is completed to be certain that students are staying on task and locating sufficient information.

Activities

Activity One

There are several suggested topics for research. Through brainstorming and discussion, by the time you distribute the first activity sheet students should have some idea of what they want to research. Students should understand that they will be using newspapers for contemporary information and other resources for historical information. Other topics that can be substituted or added include transportation, the rise of labor unions, inventions, consumerism, sports, and entertainment.

Meet with each group to be sure that all the students understand the assignment and have developed research questions broad enough to find enough information and that each student within the group is researching the topic from a different perspective.

All titles and authors of the books used should be listed in a bibliography kept in the journal. Students will write summaries of all the relevant information they find from all sources, and these summaries will be rewritten as news articles and used for the class newspaper. Web sites are available at the end of the chapter.

When you are satisfied that all students understand the assignment and have enough materials available to get started, they should begin notetaking, organizing all their notes in their journals. All newspaper articles and computer printouts should be kept in the journals along with the summaries, to make your assessment easier. Any photos, illustrations, and other materials should also be kept in the journal. As students read about the topic they may want to modify or change their original questions. They should get your approval before doing this.

Activity Two

Students will read both print and online newspapers to find articles about the research topic. If the parts of a newspaper and of news articles are old hat to your students, use the first part of this activity sheet for class discussion and review. Each student is responsible for finding and analyzing three news articles, at least one of which should be from a print newspaper. A separate activity sheet should be used for each article or printout and be stapled to the article or printout to make your assessment easier. All articles should be summarized using the questions from the activity sheet and should be evaluated for accuracy. The names of the newspapers used should be listed in the bibliography along with the addresses of any Web sites.

Activity Three

Biographies can be assigned in either of two ways, depending on the ability of your students. You may want each student to read two biographies of people of importance to the topic being researched, each from a different era. Or you may want to assign one biography to each student within the group. Students should look for these biographies online only when they have exhausted all print possibilities. All the summaries should be written as a news article about the person as if he or she is still alive or presently in the news even if the person is long since gone.

Activity Four

The activity is divided into group and class tasks. Every group will have an editor-in-chief and a political columnist, and each student should write a letter to the editor commenting on some aspect of one of the topics. Students should each contribute three summaries from the research, all to be rewritten as news articles, and from the submissions the best ones should be chosen for the final edition. Each group should present their research to the entire class for discussion. You may want to send the finished product to your local newspaper.

ASSESSMENT CHECKLIST

Student's Name _____ Class _____ Date _____

Activity Sheet 3-1   Date Checked _____

▶ Did the student:

✓ fully understand the assignment? YES __ NO __

✓ select a research topic? YES __ NO __

✓ develop appropriate research questions? YES __ NO __

✓ have a journal prepared and well-organized to begin the project? YES __ NO __

✓ understand the assessment criteria? YES __ NO __

✓ begin to list titles and authors of print resources? YES __ NO __

✓ begin to contact other appropriate sources? YES __ NO __

▶ The student is permitted to go on to Activity 3-2. YES __ NO __

▶ If the student is not permitted to continue, note the areas of concern and further work that needs to be done.

_____

_____

_____

Activity Sheet 3-2   Date Checked _____

▶ Did the student:

✓ start the research? YES __ NO __

✓ continue to maintain a well-organized journal? YES __ NO __

✓ summarize the notes using who, what, where, when, and how in preparation for writing the articles for the newspaper? YES __ NO __

✓ take part in the classroom discussion? YES __ NO __

▶ Does the bibliography include the titles of books the student has read thus far? YES __ NO __

▶ Was each of the three articles or printouts stapled to the back of the appropriate activity sheet? YES __ NO __

▶ Were all the articles summarized using the questions from the activity sheet? YES __ NO __

▶ Were the newspaper articles relevant to the assignment? YES __ NO __

▶ Were the names of the newspapers used listed in the bibliography along with the addresses of any Web sites? YES __ NO __

▸ Was the comparison of print and online newspapers complete and did it indicate understanding of the differences? YES __ NO __

▸ The student is permitted to go on to Activity 3-3. YES __ NO __

▸ If the student is not permitted to continue, note the areas of concern and further work that needs to be done.

_____

_____

_____

Activity Sheet 3-3   Date Checked _____

▸ Did the student:

    ✓ select biographies appropriate to the assignment? YES __ NO __

    ✓ complete reading two biographies of people from the different eras? YES __ NO __

    ✓ answer all the questions on the activity sheet? YES __ NO __

    ✓ compare the lives and events of the people prominent in the field he or she is researching? YES __ NO __

    ✓ demonstrate an understanding of the important contribution of these individuals? YES __ NO __

    ✓ write a news article about these people as if they are presently alive? YES __ NO __

    ✓ continue to list the research materials in a bibliography? YES __ NO __

▸ Did the news article include all the parts asked for? YES __ NO __

▸ The student is permitted to go on to Activity 3-4. YES __ NO __

▸ If the student is not permitted to continue, note the areas of concern and further work that needs to be done.

_____

_____

_____

Activity Sheet 3-4   Date Checked _____

▸ Did the student

    ✓ contribute to the group and class discussions? YES __ NO __

    ✓ participate in the group evaluation and offer constructive criticism? YES __ NO __

    ✓ contribute at least three news articles to the class newspaper? YES __ NO __

    ✓ fulfill his or her group and class tasks? YES __ NO __

▸ Were the articles from the biographies, a newspaper, and one other source? YES __ NO __

▸ Were the articles written as if the event described was a late-breaking news item? YES __ NO __

➥ Did each article have a headline, a byline, and a lead paragraph that answered the who, what, why, and when questions? YES __ NO __

Final Assessment   Date _____

➥ Did the student:

✓ complete all the activity sheets and enter the answers in the proper place in the journal? YES __ NO __

✓ contribute news articles to the class newspaper that indicate an understanding of the assignment? YES __ NO __

✓ participate in and contribute to group and class discussions and evaluations? YES __ NO __

✓ engage in critical group and class discussions about which articles to include in the newspaper? YES __ NO __

✓ fulfill all group and class assignments in a responsible manner, making positive suggestions? YES __ NO __

✓ complete the following required written reports? YES __ NO __

- Activity 3-2: Summaries of each of the three articles using who, what, when, where, why, and how, that include the main idea of the article and all the facts.

- Activity 3-3: News articles comparing each person whose biography he or she read, written as if the events that made the person famous were taking place at the present time and including headlines, lead paragraphs, the body, and a final paragraph.

FINAL GRADE _____

NOTES _____

_____

▶▶◀

ACTIVITY SHEET 3-1
PLANNING YOUR RESEARCH

In class you've started to discuss the problems and challenges that existed at the turn of the century, and realize some of the similarities to our own times, and have started to gather newspapers and read books about the subject.

Vocabulary

▶▶ agrarian

▶▶ prominent

▶▶ relevant

Understanding the Assignment

Each group of students will select a topic from the suggested list. You'll need information about how the topic concerns us at the present time to be able to compare contemporary society with that of the late nineteenth century.

You'll also need historical information about the topic as it concerned people at the end of the nineteenth century. How did the events and people of the late nineteenth century influence the modern era?

Each student will read biographies of prominent people from both eras. A class newspaper will be created using summaries from all the resources that you will write as news articles.

Each student will keep all the information he or she finds in a journal. Be sure to keep a bibliography of all the material you use.

Suggested Research Topics

▶ **Immigration**. This was an important issue during the close of the nineteenth century, just as it is today.

▶ **Role of women**. Were women's lives at the close of the nineteenth century similar to or very different from what they are today?

▶ **Industrialization**. What problems arose because of the changes from an agrarian society to an industrial one? How does this compare with what is happening at the present time?

▶ **Urban growth**. Where did the poorest people live? Have any of the problems of poverty been solved? If so, how?

▶ **Rise of big business**. Who were some of the millionaires of that era, and in what industries did they acquire their wealth? Is there a home in your area that once belonged to a millionaire? What is it used for these days? What technological advances are producing millionaires these days?

▶ **Racism**. Racism was rampant in the late nineteenth century. Has this problem been eliminated in modern society? Explain.

▶ **Conservation and pollution**. The close of the nineteenth century brought a new interest in saving land and in industrial pollution. Compare the problems of conservation and pollution by industry at the turn of the century with the problems of pollution in modern society. Will this problem be solved in the future? How?

List other topics of interest about this period of history that you want to investigate to compare with present-day society. Check with your teacher before beginning the research.

What Information Do You Need?

List everything that each member of your group already knows about the topic that your group is researching.

List the information needed to complete the assignment. Using what, who, where, why, when, and how questions can be helpful.

Each member of your group should develop at least three questions to begin your research. Brainstorm with your group, discuss the part of the topic that each student will research, and list your questions here.

_____

_____

_____

Be sure the questions are broad enough to find enough information about the topic.

Often as you do research you'll find interesting information that doesn't answer any of your questions, but is something you'd like to find out more about. That's okay, just add this information to the proper place in your journal.

Where Will You Find the Information?

Historical Information

▶ **Internet**. Online encyclopedias and other Web sites with historical information.

▶ **Library media center**. Nonfiction books, CD-ROM and print encyclopedias for background information.

▶ **Local historical societies**. Your local historical society may have primary sources such as old photographs that you can copy and put into your journal.

Information About Modern Society

▶ **Library media center**. Nonfiction books, CD-ROM and print encyclopedias for background information.

▶ **Biographies and autobiographies of prominent people**.

▶ **Current newspapers**.

▶ **Internet**. Local and national newspapers.

▶ **Interviews**. People such as recent immigrants, workers in new industries, workers who have lost their jobs because of changing times, and activists, such as people in the women's movement, and conservationists, can all be sources of information.

▶ List other sources here.

How Your Grade Will Be Determined

▶ Completion of all the activity sheets, with answers entered in the proper place in the journal.

▶ News articles contributed to the class newspaper that indicate an understanding of the assignment.

▶ Your participation and contribution to group and class discussions and evaluations.

▶ Fulfillment of all group and class assignments in a responsible manner.

▶ Completion of all the following required written reports:

Activity 3-2: Summaries of each of the three articles, using who, what, when, where, why, and how. Be sure to include the main idea of the article and all the facts you learned from it.

Activity 3-3: News articles comparing each person whose biography you have read, written as if the events that made the person famous were taking place at the present time. Remember to include headlines, lead paragraphs, the body, and a final paragraph.

ACTIVITY SHEET 3-2
USING NEWSPAPERS

Newspapers have been around for hundreds of years, and even with the development of television and computers they are still an important way to get information about current news events. They are inexpensive, easy to carry around, and provide us with lots of features that we all enjoy reading.

These days almost all large newspapers have online editions as well. These newspapers are very similar to the print edition, but they often include additional features. For this project, in addition to other resources, you'll use both print and online newspapers to find articles to answer your research questions.

Vocabulary

- caption
- feature
- pertain
- political
- revenue

Staple this activity sheet, along with the answers to the questions, in the proper place in your journal.

Parts of a Newspaper

- **Headlines**. Words printed in large type across the top of a newspaper article to catch the reader's attention.

- **Top story**. The most important article of the day, given the biggest headline. How do you think the editor decides which is the top story of the day?

  _____

  _____

- **Byline**. Tells who wrote the article.

- **Editorial**. An article that expresses the opinions of the editors of the newspaper.

- **Letters to the editor**. Give readers an opportunity to express their opinions about an issue.

- **Political columns**. Found on the editorial page. They are written by experts who give their opinions about political events.

- **Political cartoons**. Appear on the editorial page.

- **Photographs**. Find a photograph pertaining to your topic. What is the caption? Explain how it helps the reader understand the story.

  _____

  _____

▶ **Advertising**. The major source of revenue for all newspapers. There are usually two kinds of advertising in newspapers. Name them.

_____

_____

Parts of a News Article

▶ **Lead**. In the first paragraphs of a news article the reporter tries to get the reader interested in the story. All news articles have leads that summarize the story by answering some of the questions: who, what, when, where, why, and how.

▶ **Body**. The body of the article describes all the important facts in detail.

Analyzing News Articles

Topic your group is researching: _____

Each member of your group is going to find at least *three articles* about your topic from both print and online newspapers. At least one of these must be from a print newspaper.

Use a separate activity sheet for each article and attach the article from the print newspaper or the computer printout to the activity sheet. If you come across something that someone else in your group or class can use, give it to that person, and tell him or her where and when you found it. If you find something of interest to you on the topic but that is not exactly an answer to one of your questions, add it to your journal in the proper category.

▶ Name and date of the print newspaper in which you found information about your topic.

_____

▶ Name, date, and Web address of the online newspaper in which you found information about your topic.

_____

Be sure to list the names of these newspapers in your bibliography. Carefully read each article or printout and enter in your journal as much of the following information as possible:

➤ What is the event described in this article?

➤ Who are the people involved in the story?

➤ When did this event take place?

➤ Where did it take place?

➤ Why did it happen?

➤ How did it happen?

➤ What is the main idea of the story?

➤ List three facts that you learned from the story.

_____

_____

_____

Write a summary of each article using who, what, when, where, why, and how. Be sure to include the main idea of the article and all the facts you learned from it.

An opinion tells how a person feels about something, but a fact can be proven. A fact can be turned into an opinion with the addition of a few words.

Can you find any opinions about your topic from other parts of the newspapers? Circle the ones you found:

> ▶ Editorial

> ▶ Letter to the editor

> ▶ Political column

> ▶ Political cartoon

Explain how the cartoonist expresses his or her opinion.

Did you find other information related to your topic that you were able to use? Do you need to change your research question? Do you want to add any additional questions? List any additional questions or changes here.

_____

_____

Comparison of Print and Online Newspapers

Answer these questions in your journal:

➤ In which print newspaper did you find the best information?

➤ In which online newspaper did you find the best information?

➤ What are the similarities between online and print newspapers?

➤ What are the differences between the two?

➤ Which newspaper is easier to use? Explain.

➤ Which kind of newspaper had more features that you enjoy reading?

➤ Which had later-breaking stories?

Continue making notes and summarizing using all the print and nonprint resources. List every source you use in your bibliography. Discard any information that you don't need.

▶▏ ▬▬▬▬▬▬▬▬▬

ACTIVITY SHEET 3-3
READING BIOGRAPHIES

By now you have lots of information in your journal about your topic from many resources, and you've completed the newspaper assignment. You may have read about some prominent people from both the turn of the nineteenth century and modern society who were involved in the issue you are studying.

An individual biography tells the life story of one person. A collective biography contains many biographies of people who have something in common. An autobiography is written by the person. If you find a collective biography about people important to your subject, look in the table of contents to find other notable people for your topic.

Each student will read two biographies, of people important to your topic, one of whom lived at the turn of the nineteenth century and someone active at the present time. You'll then compare their lives to see what events led to their prominence. Check with your teacher before you begin reading. Each member of the group should find different people to read about.

Following are a few suggestions, but there are many more possibilities. Look for biographical information in your school library. If you have difficulty finding print material, your teacher or librarian will give you Web sites that may help you.

Be sure to staple this activity sheet into your journal.

 ▶ **Urban development**: Upton Sinclair, Jacob Riis, Lincoln Steffens, Lewis Hine, and Ida Tarbell

 ▶ **Conservation**: John Muir

 ▶ **Immigration**: Jane Addams, Jacob Riis

 Name of each person whose biography you are reading:

 _____

 _____

Provide the following information for *each biography* and enter the answers in your journal.

 ▶ About the Book.

   ✓ TITLE: _____

   ✓ AUTHOR: _____

   ✓ PUBLISHER: _____

   ✓ PUBLICATION: _____

   ✓ DATE: _____

   ✓ Is there a *bibliography* in this book?

    ✓ If there is, list the titles of any additional books that may help you find needed information.

    ✓ List the places where the author found information.

▶ About the Person:

When and where was this person born?

Is this person still alive?

Describe the events that took place that influenced the person.

Who had the greatest influence on this person?

What is this person famous for?

Add any further information that you think is important.

Write a news article about each of these people as if he or she is in the news now. Describe in vivid language the events that made each person famous as if these events were taking place at the present time. Compare their lives and the events that made each of them famous.

Remember to include headlines, lead paragraphs, the body, and a final paragraph. These articles will be used for your class newspaper.

ACTIVITY SHEET 3-4
CREATING A CLASS NEWSPAPER

Before you meet with your group to discuss the class newspaper, make sure that all summaries made from all your resources, the news article written from the biographies, and the bibliographies are complete, and everything in your journal is properly organized.

Meet with your group, exchange journals, review, and evaluate all the material that all members of the group have in their journals. Discuss which pieces of information can be discarded and what, if anything, is still needed. After the group meetings the entire class will confer about the organization of the newspaper, exchange information, and discuss and evaluate the research done by each group.

Vocabulary

- catchy
- confer
- format
- generates
- masthead
- oversee

Organization

Your newspaper will include articles, illustrations, and, if you have the proper equipment, photographs about both events that took place at the end of the nineteenth century and events that are taking place at the present time.

You can publish two editions of your newspaper with articles from each era in separate editions. Or you can publish one edition that includes articles from both eras side by side. Brainstorm with the class to see if anyone has other ideas about how to organize it. Remember, everything that you include must be news from both eras written as if it just happened.

The Newspaper

Each student will contribute at least three news articles to the class newspaper.

One article should be from the print or online newspaper articles, one from the biographies, and the third from other sources.

All the articles, including the information from the biographies, must be written as if these events are late-breaking news. Each article should have a headline, a byline, a lead paragraph, a body, and a closing paragraph. It should answer as many of the who, what, when, where, why, and how questions as possible.

Members of the group may have used the same resources. Review the bibliographies and use each entry only once. Your group will evaluate the articles to decide which should be submitted for the final edition of the class publication.

Which of the news articles will your group submit for the newspaper? Following are some of the criteria to use:

➤ Is the information in the article accurate?

➤ Does it include a bibliographic reference that tells where the information came from?

➤ Does the article have a headline that catches your attention?

➤ Does the lead begin to answer the who, what, where, when, and why questions?

➤ Are all the facts included in the body of the article?

➤ If this article expresses an opinion, does the writer give reasons and facts to back up the opinion?

➤ Has the article been typed up on a computer and checked for spelling?

➤ If the information came from a Web site, is the Web address included in the bibliography?

Group Tasks

At least one member of each group should be a political columnist and should write an opinion about the topic.

Each group will choose an editor-in-chief to oversee the group's part of the production and make sure that all deadlines are met. The editor-in-chief of each group will decide with the teacher which of the articles will be included for the final edition. Letters should be written by each student in the group commenting on and offering opinions about one of the researched topics other than his or her own.

Class Tasks

One or two students in the class should be appointed to the following positions:

➤ **Layout editor**. Will decide how the newspaper is to be arranged. After the editors discuss their ideas for the format their views should be presented to the entire class and the teacher for final approval.

➤ **Copy editor**. Proofreads everything and checks the accuracy of articles. At least two students selected by the teacher should be in charge of this.

➤ **Local editor**. Is in charge of reports on news of importance to your city or town. Do any of the research topics apply to an issue of local importance?

➤ **Business editor**. Is in charge of news of importance to the business world. Which group do you think should be in charge of business writing?

▶ **Features editors**. Are in charge of fashion, music, and sports items. Can you think of any other features to include?

▶ **Editorial writers**. Comment on the similarities and differences of the two eras before the newspaper is printed, and after all the groups have exchanged information.

▶ **Letters-to-the-editor editor**. Chooses the best of the letters to the editor for publication.

Final Decisions

Don't forget your newspaper needs a catchy name. What do you think describes it best?

It also needs a masthead that includes the names of all the students and their positions on the paper. Brainstorm with the entire class to decide on the masthead for your newspaper.

Will your class accept advertising? If so, what kind?

What are some of the other features you would like to include? All the features must have a basis for comparing the two eras. Fashion, sports, and entertainment are permissible if a group has researched these topics, but horoscopes would be a no-no! Sorry!

If the class decides to include puzzles, ask your teacher or librarian for a Web site that generates puzzles.

WEB SITES

A & E Television Networks. *Biography.com*. © 2000. Available: www.biography.com. (Accessed October 17, 2000).
Short biographies both past and present.

The American Experience. *Wayback—Stand Up for Your Rights*. © 1998/1999. Available: www.pbs.org/wgbh/amex/kids/civilrights/. (Accessed October 17, 2000).
Covers religious freedom, women and the vote, and school desegregation. Loaded with information plus photos, games, quizzes, and interviews. If you can access only one site, make it this one.

The American Experience. *The Richest Man in the World: Andrew Carnegie*. © 1998/1999 WGBH Educational Foundation. Available: www.pbs.org/wgbh/amex/carnegie. (Accessed October 17, 2000).
Check out all the links for great information about business and millionaires during this era.

American Memory Library of Congress. *African American Perspectives*. Updated October 19, 1998. Available: http://memory.loc.gov .ammem/aap/aaphome.html. (Accessed October 17, 2000).
African-American history and culture from the early nineteenth through early twentieth centuries, with most materials published between 1875 and 1900.

Edmonds School District Lynnwood, WA. *American History*. Updated October 14, 2000. Available: http://dent.edmonds .wednet/IMD/historyamerican.html. (Accessed October 17, 2000).
This is a massive list of links for every possible aspect of American history. Access before your students do to save time.

Ellis Island. n.d. Available: www.ellisisland .org/. (Accessed October 17, 2000).
The place to begin a search for material about immigration. Includes the Immigration History Center, Ellis Island Museum, and links to other sources.

Gallery of Achievement. © 2000. Available: www .achievement.org/galleryachieve.html. (Accessed October 17, 2000).
Arranged by Hall of Arts, Business, Sports, Public Service, and Science and Exploration. The focus is on "individuals who have shaped the twentieth century by their achievements." Biographies, profiles, and interviews with Academy inductees.

Immigration Facts. n.d. Available: www .immigrationforum.org/Facts/default.htm. (Accessed October 17, 2000).
Provides a "variety of immigration information" including current immigration issues, immigrants in the news, and an immigration chronology.

Institute for African American Studies, University of Georgia. *African American in History*. © 1996. Available: www.uga .edu/ ~ iaas/History.html. (Accessed October 17, 2000).
One of many excellent sites devoted to African Americans. These are short biographies of both historical and contemporary figures.

Internet Public Library. *Reading Room Newspapers*. Updated October 14, 2000. Available: www.ipl.org/reading/news/. (Accessed October 17, 2000).
Includes newspapers from every state in the United States.

Learning Page of the Library of Congress: Journalism, Journalist. Updated June 2000. Available: http://memory.loc.gov /ammem/ndlpedu/keywords/journali.html. (Accessed October 17, 2000).
Includes African American Perspectives, 1818–1907, Evolution of the Conservation Movement, and Votes for Women 1848–1921.

National Archives and Records Administration. *The Woman Suffrage Movement*. Updated February 4, 1998. Available: www.nara .gov/education/teaching/woman/home .html. (Accessed October 17, 2000).
Documents, background, images, and classroom activities related to the women's movement.

The National Park Service. *Ellis Island*. n.d. Available: www.nps.gov/stli/serv02.htm. (Accessed October 17, 2000).
Complete history of Ellis Island, museum exhibits, collections, and archives.

The National Women's Hall of Fame. © 1998–2000. Available: http://greatwomen.org. (Accessed October 17, 2000).
Outstanding site from The National Women's Hall of Fame in Seneca Falls, New York.

Neary, Walter. *Journalism: History Links*. Updated July 1999. Available: http://members.aol.com/Nearys/journhist.html. (Accessed October 17, 2000).
History of journalists back to the colonial period. Includes material from individual states.

Recommended Websites for Student Researchers. *Race and Race Relations in America*. © 1997–2000. Available: www.newhorizons.org/announce_phsrace.html. (Accessed October 17, 2000).
From New Horizons; several excellent links to information on race relations, including text documents and audio clips of civil rights leaders.

Schultz, Stanley K., Professor of History. *Who's Who In American History*. © 1999 University of Wisconsin Board of Regents. Available: http://us.history.wisc.edu/hist102/bios.html. (Accessed October 17, 2000).
Search by name, era, or occupation for people prominent in American history.

Sher, Julian. *U.S. Papers*. © 1999. Available: www.journalismnet.com/uspapers.htm. (Accessed October 17, 2000).
Links to many important American national publications, weeklies, and news services. Includes archives and "story beats" on such topics as women, environment, and culture.

Smithsonian Institute *Sweatshop Exhibit*. n.d. Available: http://americanhistory.si.edu/sweatshops/index.htm. (Accessed October 17, 2000).
Lots of information and graphics about the history of sweatshops in the United States.

Tenement Museum. *The Tenement as History and Housing*. Limmer, Ruth & Dolkart, Andrew S. n.d. Available: www.wnet.org/archive/tenement/eagle.html. (Accessed October 17, 2000).
A history of urban housing with photos of actual tenements; describes living conditions and laws that had an impact on urban dwellings.

Welcome to Angel Island Immigration Station Foundation. *Asian History, Chinese History, Chinese Americans*. © 1995–2000. Updated October 8, 2000 Mel Wong. Available: www.a-bctter.com/asians.htm. (Accessed October 17, 2000).
The place to find information about Asian history and immigration.

Chapter Four

COME TO THE FAIR!

The World's Columbian Exposition, held in Chicago in 1893, commemorated the 400th anniversary of Columbus's discovery of the New World, and is considered by many historians to be the greatest American fair of them all. It was visited by millions of people who came from all over the world to view its wonders.

It was the perfect place to go to explore how America had changed in the last decades of the nineteenth century, and it remains a perfect "place" for students to learn how historic events often affect their own lives.

The fair had a great influence on architecture, technology, commerce, and popular culture as the country moved from an agrarian society to an industrial one. The acceptance and celebration of consumption and technology was the most significant and lasting impact of the fair.

Cracker Jack, picture postcards, hamburgers, carbonated soda, the Ferris wheel, and the zipper were all introduced at the fair, as was the "Pledge of Allegiance," copies of which were sent to teachers for recital the morning of the opening of the fair. People were awed by the possibilities of the new technology, and amazed by the more than 125,000 electric lights displayed at the fair. The White City at the fair inspired L. Frank Baum to write about the Emerald City in the Oz books. John Philip Sousa marches were performed by the many bands on the fairgrounds, Dvorak composed the New World Symphony in honor of the Exposition, and Scott Joplin developed ragtime music while working at the fair. As if all this wasn't enough, the Exposition introduced a new holiday, Columbus Day, and contributed to urban planning and beaux-arts architecture, which became the standard form used in public buildings for many years and in the plans for Washington, D.C.

Fairs are a reflection of the times in which they take place. The World's Columbian Exposition was no exception. It took place during an era of societal change very similar to our own times, and its influence and legacy are ingrained in modern American culture. The fair exemplified the ways in which America was transforming from a producer to a consumer society. Visitors to the fair were enticed by a great variety of concessions selling all kinds of goods, and the equating of consuming with fun is still alive and well in shopping malls all across America. Enjoying oneself became forever tied to making purchases and spending money. The move to a consumer-based society was accompanied by an extraordinary growth of corporations and the rise of millionaires as well as incredible destitution in both rural areas and in the slums of the growing cities.

Students will research the significance of the legacies of the fair that still affect our lives today. They will learn about its relevance to us, enabling them to understand that what they experience today did not just rise from nowhere: even such things as shopping malls, carnival midways, and Disneyland have historic roots. The class will plan and build a class fair modeled on the one in 1893. They will apply the information gleaned from the research to make decisions about what objects to include that will exemplify the changes taking place in society at the present time as well as to consider what objects will change their own lives well into the twenty-first century.

This chapter can be used along with **Chapter Three**, "America at the Turn of the Centuries," which emphasizes other topics of the same period.

PROCEDURE

Materials

Photographs from the 1890s, maps and books about the fair, photos and books of more recent fairs, Sears Roebuck catalog 1890 edition, other old catalogs available from Dover Press and the public library, time travel fiction, word processing software

Equipment

Computer with Internet access

Curriculum Connections

Language arts, social studies, science, technology

Objectives

Students will:

▶ recognize how contemporary life is related to past events.

▶ compare and contrast elements of the fair to determine similarities to and differences from our own times.

▶ apply the elements present at the fair to personal experience.

▶ apply the model of the fair to create their own class fair.

▶ determine what significant objects to include in the class fair.

▶ write a group story based on the completed research.

▶ locate primary resources pertaining to the community from the local historical society.

▶ summarize notes from many sources and enter them into the proper categories in their journals.

▶ organize individual journal entries into categories of information.

Preparation

Begin by asking if any students have ever visited a Disney theme park, read the Oz books, taken a ride on a Ferris wheel, attended a carnival, eaten a hamburger, sipped a soda, recited the "Pledge of Allegiance," or watched a Columbus Day parade. Explain to the class that all of the above had their start at the World's Columbian Exposition, held in Chicago in 1893.

Have pictures available of beaux-arts buildings in your area and ask if anyone has ever visited a place that resembles the pictures. Perhaps some of your students have been to Washington, D.C., and can describe some of the beaux-arts buildings they visited there.

Ask what students think the world was like 100 years ago. How did people entertain themselves? Discuss the various aspects of the fair so that they may begin thinking about the topics they want to research and how those relate to their own lives. Old catalogs are invaluable for this project. Students who choose to research business, advertising, and consumerism can begin to understand how these mail-order catalogs created and filled a need for products in areas where they were not previously available. The catalogs can also be used for the technology and invention topic as students can compare technology of yesteryear with today.

Activities

Activity One

The first activity explains what the project entails and details the possible research topics. After students read and understand the assignment, divide the class into groups. If students opt to research a topic not on this sheet, be sure that enough sources are available for them to find the information. If possible, either make a visit to your local historical society or invite a speaker who can tell the class about the community's past and also show them some photos.

Activity Two

Once research has started, students should answer the questions in this activity to be sure that they have gathered enough information. Lessons for notetaking, research, and summarizing appear in **Chapter Nine**. Divide the questions among the students in each group. Students should be reminded to staple activity sheets into their journals along with the answers to the questions, to make life easier for you.

Activity Three

Each student will be responsible for writing only a part of a story. However, if there are students who insist on writing their own complete stories, don't discourage them from doing so. Each group's story should encompass only the research they completed for their chosen topic, using information they have gathered plus their imaginations. These stories will be included as part of the class fair, and you might want to tape them. After each group evaluates their story they should read it aloud to the class, and the other students should make suggestions for improving them. After all the editing is complete have someone from each group use the computer to type up the stories for distribution to all the groups as well as to visitors to the fair.

Activity Four

The fair can be an elaborate, end-of-year affair or something simpler held in a corridor or entrance way. The class should have lots of material to display. Laminate as much as possible if you can. If possible, see if you can borrow some old toys or games. Someone may even have an old phonograph or telephone or some other piece of equipment lying around a garage or attic. These objects will add lots of interest to the fair. If you have the energy and the room, it would be nice to have kids selling stuff in booths, trying to replicate the fair. If you have some talented students who can make a model or illustrations of the buildings or midway, that would be great also. Music will add to the festivities as well. Some Sousa marches will add to the atmosphere.

The stories and spiffed-up journals should be on display. It might also be fun to have a questionnaire for visitors asking what their predictions are for the future.

ASSESSMENT CHECKLIST

Student's Name _____ Class _____ Date _____

Activity Sheet 4-1   Date Checked _____

➤ Did the student

    ✓ fully understand the assignment? YES __ NO __

    ✓ select a research topic and join a group? YES __ NO __

    ✓ develop appropriate research questions? YES __ NO __

    ✓ begin to list titles and authors of print resources? YES __ NO __

    ✓ begin to contact other appropriate sources? YES __ NO __

    ✓ prepare a journal that is well-organized into categories? YES __ NO __

    ✓ understand the assessment criteria? YES __ NO __

➤ The student is permitted to go on to Activity 4-2. YES __ NO __

➤ If the student is not permitted to continue, note the areas of concern and further work that needs to be done.

_____

_____

_____

Activity Sheet 4-2   Date Checked _____

➤ Did the student:

    ✓ use a variety of both print and online resources? YES __ NO __

    ✓ summarize notes using who, what, where, when? YES __ NO __

    ✓ begin to list resources in the bibliography? YES __ NO __

    ✓ answer all the assigned questions? YES __ NO __

    ✓ staple the activity sheet in the proper place in the journal? YES __ NO __

➤ The student is permitted to go on to Activity 4-3. YES __ NO __

➤ If the student is not permitted to continue, note the areas of concern and further work that needs to be done.

_____

_____

_____

Activity Sheet 4-3   Date Checked _____

➤ Did the student:

    ✓ participate in group discussion prior to starting the story? YES __ NO __

    ✓ base his or her part of the story on actual facts found through research? YES __ NO __

    ✓ complete his or her part of the story? YES __ NO __

    ✓ answer all the assigned questions on the activity sheet? YES __ NO __

    ✓ continue to list the research materials in a bibliography? YES __ NO __

    ✓ participate in the evaluation of the story and contribute to the writing of the final story? YES __ NO __

➤ The student is permitted to go on to Activity 4-4. YES __ NO __

➤ If the student is not permitted to continue, note the areas of concern and further work that needs to be done.

_____

_____

_____

Activity Sheet 4-4   Date Checked _____

➤ Did the student:

    ✓ contribute significant suggestions to group and class discussions? YES __ NO __

    ✓ offer meaningful suggestions about organization and displays? YES __ NO __

Final Assessment   Date _____

➤ Did the student:

    ✓ contribute meaningful suggestions to all class and group discussions? YES __ NO __

    ✓ use many, varied, and appropriate sources? YES __ NO __

    ✓ complete all the activity sheets and staple them neatly into the journal with the completed answers to all the questions? YES __ NO __

    ✓ complete the journal with information divided into appropriate categories and include an illustrated cover, title page, table of contents, and captioned photos and illustrations? YES __ NO __

    ✓ contribute to the group story using vivid language in a way that indicated an understanding of the assignment? YES __ NO __

    ✓ fulfill the assigned task during the class fair responsibly and completely? YES __ NO __

FINAL GRADE _____

    NOTES _____

_____

▶▶| ▬▬▬▬▬▬▬▬▬▬▬▬▬▬▬▬

ACTIVITY SHEET 4-1
PLANNING YOUR RESEARCH

Every time you take a ride on a Ferris wheel, enjoy a carnival midway, send a picture postcard to a friend, visit an art museum, turn on the lights, go to the movies, or recite the "Pledge of Allegiance" you are experiencing something that was first introduced at the World's Columbian Exposition of 1893.

Although the theme of this Exposition was supposed to be the commemoration of the 400th anniversary of Columbus's discovery of the New World, it was actually a symbol of the movement from an agrarian to an industrial society and a new dependence on manufactured products, with influences that are still felt today.

Vocabulary

➡ exposition

➡ legacy

➡ prevalent

The Assignment

The class will be divided into groups depending on the topic you choose to research.

There are three parts to the research:

> ▶ The fair and its legacy.

> ▶ A description of how the things introduced at the fair affected your community during the twentieth century.

> ▶ The predictions you make for changes to your community during the twenty-first century.

After the research is complete, each student will write part of a time travel group story that takes a person from your community to the World's Columbian Exposition in 1893 and into the future.

After the research is complete the class will develop a fair modeled on the World's Columbian Exposition. The fair will include all the completed research, your stories, and photos and any other primary source material you find.

All the information you find should be kept in individual journals divided into categories of information. The journal should have an illustrated cover, a table of contents, a title page, and a bibliography of all the material you used.

What Information Do You Need?

Brainstorm with your group and list everything that each member of your group already knows about the topic that your group is researching.

List the information you need to complete the assignment. Using what, who, where, when, and how questions can be helpful. Some suggestions follow:

▶ **Technology and inventions**. What technology was introduced at the fair, and how did it change life in your community during the twentieth century?

▶ **Consumerism**. How did consumerism affect the lifestyle of your community during the twentieth century?

▶ **Entertainment**. Describe the entertainment and amusements on the Exposition's midway.

▶ **Architecture**. What impact did the architecture of the fair have on buildings during the twentieth century in your community?

List other topics of interest about the fair and its influence on twentieth-century America that you may want to research. Discuss them with your teacher to be certain that there are enough resources available to find the needed information.

As you do your research, make notes, summarize each resource you use, and enter the information into the proper category in your journal.

Where Will You Find the Information?

▶ **Internet**. Online encyclopedias for background information. Your teacher will give you a list of Web sites to search for additional information about the Exposition and the topic your group is researching.

▶ **Library media center**. Nonfiction books, CD-ROM and print encyclopedias for background material, fiction books about time travel.

▶ **Historical society**. Photographs and other primary source material about how your local community has changed during the twentieth century.

What other sources might be able to provide information?

How Your Grade Will Be Determined

▶ Meaningful participation in all class and group discussion.

▶ All activity sheets stapled neatly into the journal, with the answers to all the questions.

▶ A journal divided into categories of information, with an illustrated cover, a table of contents, a title page, and a bibliography of all the material you use.

▶ Your contribution to the group story that is based on your research and uses vivid language to describe the fair, the visitor, and the visit.

▶ Your assignment during the class fair, fulfilled responsibly and completely.

▸▸▎ ▃▃▃▃▃▃▃▃▃▃▃▃▃▃▃▃▃▃▃▃

ACTIVITY SHEET 4-2
THE FAIR'S LEGACY AND YOUR COMMUNITY

Use the notes and summaries in your journals to answer the questions in this activity *only for the topic your group is researching*. Be sure to add any additional information you found through your research. Divide the questions among the students in your group.

Vocabulary

▸▸ consumerism

▸▸ prominent

▸▸ spectator

Be sure to staple this activity sheet into your journal. Enter your answers to the questions in the proper place in the journal.

Architecture

▶ **The fair**. Describe the architecture and architects who were prominent at the fair.

What was the *White City?*

How did the *World's Columbian Exposition* influence architecture during the twentieth century?

▶ **The community**. What impact did the architecture of the fair have on buildings in your community during the twentieth century?

Are there any beaux-art buildings in your community? List them.

Describe the buildings that were prevalent in your community at the turn of the century.

How do they differ from the buildings in the community now? How are they similar?

▶ **The future**. What kinds of buildings and materials do you think will be prevalent in the future? What architectural features would you use to describe the architecture of our times to the people of the future?

Entertainment

▶ **The fair**

Describe the entertainment and amusements on the Exposition's midway.

How did the midway influence amusement parks, carnivals, and music during the twentieth century?

How did the *World's Columbian Exposition* influence entertainment and music and the things people did for fun during the twentieth century?

How did increased leisure time affect spectator sports?

▶ **The community**

Compare what you and your friends do for fun with entertainment in the late nineteenth century. List the similarities and the differences.

How did the differences affect the way people in your community lived during the twentieth century?

Are there any amusements that were available in the nineteenth century that you wish you had now?

▶ **The future**

What do you think people will do for fun later in the twenty-first century?

How do you think entertainment will be different then than it is now?

Which developments in entertainment best represent our times? Describe them for future generations.

Technology and Inventions

▶ **The fair**

What technology was introduced at the fair?

Who were the great inventors of the period?

How did these inventions influence the way people lived during the twentieth century?

▶ **The community**

List some inventions that changed the lives of people into the twentieth century.

How did these inventions and technology change the way people lived and worked in your community during the twentieth century?

▶ **The future**

Describe how new technology and inventions will change people's lives in the future.

Which inventions do you think best represent our times? How would you tell people in the future about them?

Consumerism

▶ The fair

How did the fair lead to the consumerism of the twentieth century?

What nations and businesses exhibited their goods at the fair?

Describe products that were introduced at the fair that are still used today.

▶ The community

What impact did mail order catalogs have on consumerism in America at the start of the twentieth century?

List the similarities and the differences in products and purchasing between our own times and the late nineteenth century.

How did the differences affect lifestyles in the twentieth century?

What changes came about in your community because of these differences?

Compare how you purchase clothing and other items with the way in which youngsters your age made purchases at the end of the nineteenth century.

▶ The future

What products do you predict will be popular later in the twenty-first century?

How will they change people's lives?

Do you believe mail order catalogs will continue to be important, or will a new way of buying become more popular in the twenty-first century? Explain.

What products that you think best represent our times would you introduce to people living in the future?

▶▶▏ ━━━━━━━━━━━━━━━━━━━━━━━

ACTIVITY SHEET 4-3
WRITING THE STORY

You've probably read lots of books where the main character finds a way to travel back in time or travels into the future. Each student in your group will write part of a story about a time traveler from your community going back in time to the fair, then into the future. The story must be based on facts from your research as well as on your imagination. The story will describe all the wonders this person encounters at the fair and the wonders of the future. One student may want to describe the character, another what he or she sees at the fair or how he or she got there, and someone in your group may want to travel into the future.

Before you begin, exchange, discuss, and read each other's summaries to be sure that you have enough information about both the fair and the community.

Some Things to Think About

The Protagonist

▶▶ Describe the protagonist.

▶▶ What is his or her name?

▶▶ Is the protagonist male or female?

▶▶ How old is the protagonist?

▶▶ Describe how the main character feels at the beginning of the story, before he or she goes to the fair.

▶▶ Is he or she scared, worried, happy, lucky, sad?

▶▶ Did the main character change in any way by the end of the story?

▶▶ Did the protagonist learn anything from this experience?

The Plot

▶▶ What event led to the main character going into a different time period?

▶▶ Describe what he or she sees when first arriving at the fair.

▶▶ Which "special day" at the fair did your visitor see and enjoy the most?

▶▶ What things will he or she find puzzling about it?

▶▶ Is he or she traveling alone?

➺ How did the protagonist get there? Airplane, magic carpet, boat, train?

➺ Does the protagonist want to travel to this place, or does someone else have power over him or her?

➺ Describe what the hero of the story sees or meets when he or she travels to this other time.

➺ Does the person want to go home, or would he or she prefer to stay in this place?

➺ Is the protagonist able to travel back and forth?

➺ How does he or she do this?

➺ Compare the place the protagonist came from with the place he or she travels to.

➺ Which is a better place to live? Why?

➺ Will the protagonist ever get back home?

➺ What kinds of things will he or she bring back as gifts?

➺ Based on the research you did, think about what would amaze the person at the fair the most.

Questions for Each Group

Architecture

➺ What building in your community did the protagonist leave from? Describe how this building might be similar to or different from the one he or she visits at the fair or in the future.

➺ What was the first building the visitor saw? Describe it.

➺ Which building impressed him or her most? Explain.

➺ What buildings did he or she visit and enjoy the most?

➺ What was the visitor's reaction to the White City?

Entertainment and Amusements

➺ What event did the visitor leave from?

➺ Was he or she at a ball game or on a Ferris wheel, or perhaps at a carnival?

➺ Compare how this place might be similar to or different from the fair or a place in the future.

➺ Describe some of the amusements the visitor enjoyed.

➤ What was his or her impression of the midway?

➤ Describe the music. Is it loud? Does it help the visitor get into the mood?

➤ What music did the visitor enjoy the most?

➤ Did he or she take a ride on the new Ferris wheel?

➤ What was the visitor's reaction to it?

➤ Did the visitor think that he or she wanted something like this back home?

Technology and Inventions

➤ What technology was the visitor using at the time he or she got to the fair?

➤ Describe some of the technology the visitor saw at the fair.

➤ How did the visitor react to this technology?

➤ Which technology introduced at the fair impressed the visitor the most?

➤ How did the visitor feel this new technology was going to change his or her life at home?

➤ Was the visitor able to bring the new technology home?

➤ How did the people in the community react to it?

➤ If the visitor travels into the future, describe how he or she got there.

Commerce and New Products

➤ What was the visitor doing when he or she left for the fair? Eating or shopping?

➤ Which of the new products introduced at the fair did your visitor enjoy the most?

➤ Did the visitor taste something that he or she had never tasted before? Describe how it tasted.

➤ What delicious smells were in the air? Describe them.

➤ What new product did the visitor encounter in the future?

➤ Was your visitor excited about using this new product at home?

➤ Was he or she able to bring it home?

➤ How did the people in the community react to it?

Do You Have Enough Information to Complete Your Part of the Story?

If you don't have enough information, list the items you still need. Go back to the reference source you think will provide that information or find a new resource in the library or on the Internet.

Evaluation

Exchange your part of the story with other students in your group. Each part should be read aloud, and the group should work together to decide how to put all the parts together for the final story, with all the students in the group making a contribution to it.

Copies of each story should be made for the entire class and the stories should be read and discussed in class.

The story may be taped for use at the class fair.

▶▶│ ▬▬▬▬▬▬▬▬▬▬▬▬▬▬▬▬

ACTIVITY SHEET 4-4
COME TO OUR FAIR!

It's time to begin making plans for your class fair, based on what you have learned about the World's Columbian Exposition. Everyone in the class has a journal filled with information and photographs you gathered about the fair, life at the end of the nineteenth century, and the impact of the fair on your community during the twentieth century. You also have been making predictions about what you think life will be like in the future. If you used the Internet you may have downloaded pictures. How can you apply the research the class did to create a theme for your class fair?

Vocabulary

▶▶ captioned

▶▶ concession

▶▶ exemplify

Exhibits

What exhibits will you include for your fair that will exemplify the fair, changes to your community during the twentieth century, and your predictions for the future? Brainstorm with your group and discuss which exhibits to include and how they will be organized. Afterwards the class will discuss each group's suggestions.

Consumerism

▶▶ What products will you display that were first introduced at the fair?

▶▶ Will you have concessions that sell some of these products?

▶▶ How will you advertise these products?

▶▶ What kinds of products will you display to represent the future?

▶▶ Do you have any old mail order catalogs to put on display?

▶▶ Brainstorm with your group for additional ideas.

Architecture

▶▶ Do you have photos and illustrations that highlight the building styles that were first seen at the fair?

➤ Do you have photos that show the impact of these styles on your community?

➤ Are you able to build simple models of some of these buildings or show examples of beaux-arts in your community?

➤ How will you present your ideas about styles and building materials of the future?

➤ Brainstorm with your group for additional ideas.

Entertainment

➤ Do you have photos that show any of the amusements at the fair?

➤ Will you play tapes of some of the music that was introduced at the fair?

➤ Do you have photos of some musicians who were prominent there?

➤ Does anyone have old toys or games that you can borrow and display?

➤ How will you compare what kids do for fun these days with what they did then and what you think they will do in the future?

➤ Brainstorm with your group for additional ideas.

Technology and Inventions

➤ Do you have photos of the technology and inventions that were introduced at the fair?

➤ Does anyone in the community have an old phonograph, camera, or telephone that you can borrow for this exhibit?

➤ How can you show your predictions for the future?

➤ Brainstorm with your group for additional ideas.

Other Exhibits

Each group's final story should be available and enough copies be made for your visitors.

All the journals should include an illustrated cover, a title page, a table of contents, an introduction that includes an explanation of the project, and a bibliography. All the photos should be neatly captioned.

Everything, including photos and other primary sources that show how your community changed during the twentieth century, should be displayed.

Tasks

Each student will be responsible for some part of the fair, both while it's being organized and while it's on display. Your teacher will select the students for each job.

> ▶ **Organizers**. These students will decide exactly how and where the exhibits will be displayed and make certain that everything is properly labeled and if possible laminated.

> ▶ **Conservators**. They will be in charge of keeping everything in good condition. If something is torn or lost during the exhibition, these students will be responsible for replacing and repairing it.

> ▶ **Guides**. A few students will escort visitors around the fair, explaining each exhibit.

> ▶ **Security**. Some students should watch the exhibits so that when visitors view the work they are reminded not to touch anything and are told why this is important.

> ▶ **Educators**. These students should write information about the fair, explaining the project, and distribute the material to visitors, including other classes, faculty, parents, and the community.

You might want to write and distribute a questionnaire for your visitors that asks them to make predictions about the future. When the fair is over, these can be sent to the visitors.

WEB SITES

The American Experience—America 1900. © 1999 PBS/WGBH. Available: www.pbs .org/wgbh/amex/1900. (Accessed October 20, 2000).
Biographies of twentieth-century people and events, and a search option.

The American Experience. *Wayback—US History for Kids*. © 1998/1999 WGBH Educational Foundation. Available: www .pbs.org/wgbh/amex/kids/tech/1900. (Accessed October 20, 2000).
Loads of great stuff, including music videos 1900 style, the first telephone operators, early autos, and predictions from 1900. Don't miss this one!

Chicago Historical Society. *History Files— The World's Columbian Exposition*. © 1998. Available: www.chicagohistory.net /history/expo.html. (Accessed October 20, 2000).
Lots of photos, maps, and posters, sure to grab your students. Includes a look at some of the artifacts and interesting facts about the fair.

Illinois State Museum. *At Home with Art & Industry: 1890–1920*. © December 1996. Available: www.museum.state.il.us/exhibits /athome/1890/index.html. (Accessed October 20, 2000).
Link from *At Home in the Heartland* from the Illinois State Museum. Not just for residents of Illinois. Links to mail order catalogs, objects from the past, trends in style, and price comparisons, among other subjects.

The Motion Picture, Broadcasting and Recorded Sound Division, Library of Congress. *Edison Motion Picture & Sound Recordings Inventing Entertainment*. Updated January 13, 1999. Available: http://memory.loc .gov/ammem/edhtml/edhome.html. (Accessed October 20, 2000).
"This site features 341 motion pictures, 81 disc sound recordings, and other related materials, such as photographs and original magazine articles." Certainly worth a visit.

Schulman, Bruce R. *World's Columbian Exposition: Interactive Guide to the World's Columbian Exposition*. © 1996–2000. Available: http://users.vnet.net/schulman /Columbian/columbian.html. (Accessed October 20, 2000).
Huge amount of information including illustrations, art and architecture, and legacy of the fair.

Technology Timeline. Available: www.pbs.org /wgbh/amex/technology/techtimeline /timeline/. (Accessed October 20, 2000).
Timeline of inventions, with descriptions.

World's Columbian Exposition—Idea, Experience, Aftermath. © 1996, 1997 Julie K. Rose. Available: http://xroads.virginia.edu / ~ MA96/WCE/title.html. (Accessed October 20, 2000).
Overview of the fair, with links to its legacy, reactions of visitors, and a grand tour complete with photos. Lots of great stuff.

Zwick. Jim. *World's Columbian Exposition*. © 1999–2000. Available: www.boondocksnet .com/expos /columbian.html. (Accessed October 20, 2000).
Links to articles, maps, and photos dating back to 1893 that can provide you with an overview of many aspects of the fair. Of particular interest are the links to many of the state exhibits, architecture, and technology.

Chapter Five

CAREERS: WHAT DOES THE FUTURE HOLD?

When I became a librarian years ago, the technology in the library consisted of a few tape recorders, film strip projectors, a slide projector, and an overhead projector. Who would have ever guessed that all of it would become obsolete within just a few years, and I would find myself connected to something called the Internet that would become my primary research tool? It was inconceivable.

It's important for students to understand that many of them will be doing jobs in the future that they have never even heard of. It seems hard to prepare for a job that doesn't exist, but what's crucial is for youngsters to build skills that will endure the test of time and can easily be transferred to a variety of jobs in a changing labor market. Students need to concentrate on building communication, literacy, and computer skills, as well as organizational abilities, and be capable of working in teams and have the flexibility to learn new information and adapt to change.

Using both primary and secondary sources, this chapter explores the evolution of the world of work—how it has changed in the past and the conditions that brought about that change—and relates people's experiences during the past 60 years to the present. The Library of Congress *WPA Life Histories—Home Page. Manuscripts from the Federal Writers' Project, 1936–1940* will provide primary source material through interviews with working people of the Depression era, as will interviews with older retired people in the community. Studying conditions of the past puts the present into perspective and enables students to apply that knowledge and understand more fully what is taking place in the contemporary work world.

Interviews online with experts in the student's area of interest and live interviews with people in the community will provide insight into the present work world. Secondary sources, both print and nonprint, will be searched for information relating to the student's career interest. The Internet is an ideal place for students and teachers to contact a wide variety of professionals for interviewing. By using the Internet for research and connecting through e-mail to people working in specific fields of interest, students can correspond with many people in a variety of jobs, enabling them to further explore their options.

The final project will be creating Career Day handbooks, which will include the best of the research, primary source documents, and a bibliography. These handbooks can be on display for Career Day.

PROCEDURE

Materials

Photographs of people at work, pay stubs, old newspapers and magazines, newspaper want ads, reference and history books, books about work, blank cassette tapes, student notebooks, word processing software

Equipment

Computers with e-mail and Internet access, tape recorders

Curriculum Connections

Language arts, history, technology

Objectives

Students will:

▶ identify community resources available to them.

▶ identify career possibilities.

▶ understand the changing job market, the conditions that cause these changes, and how the changes affect their career choices in the future.

▶ apply what they learn about work of the past to the present.

▶ conduct interviews with members of the community.

▶ access the Internet to find people in various occupations for interviews.

▶ locate both primary and secondary sources for research.

▶ compare and contrast primary and secondary sources.

▶ identify their talents and interests for potential career options.

▶ explore career options through online and local interviews.

▶ research using a wide variety of sources.

▶ compare and contrast past working conditions with the present.

▶ develop questions for interviews.

▶ analyze the conditions that led to changes that are occurring in the workplace.

Preparation

Discuss with the class the changes taking place in the workplace so that they will begin to understand how changes have occurred in the past, how changes continue to occur, and how they will do so in the future. Prepare a bulletin board with help wanted ads and discuss the various occupations to peak student interest as they begin to think about the careers they want to explore. Have students begin to gather newspaper and magazine articles about various jobs and changes in the work world. Invite a speaker from a volunteer organization who can turn kids on to ways that they can help their community while also learning job-related skills.

The best way for students to find information about a field that interests them is to have them talk with people in that field. Interviewees can be recruited right in your community. Try the yellow pages and the local Chamber of Commerce. One of the best career day speakers I ever heard was the president of the New York Stock Exchange, who took the time from his busy day to visit a sixth-grade class. He was a wonderful, dynamic speaker, and the students loved him.

Students will access the Internet for both primary and secondary sources. The Library of Congress *WPA Life Histories—Home Page. Manuscripts from the Federal Writers' Project, 1936–1940* provides interviews with people made during the Depression years, which can be accessed for firsthand information about many occupations as they once were. In addition, an interview with an elderly person who can provide information about how a particular career has changed or perhaps disappeared will be required as well as an interview with someone presently employed in the field of interest to the student and an online expert.

The final project will be Career Day handbooks, developed by each group. The handbooks should be centered on broad themes such as science and technology or visual and performing arts and should include the changes that have taken place in the working lives of the people interviewed as well as any artifacts and information about the specific careers each student researched. Each handbook should have an attractive cover with a title, a title page, a table of contents, any primary source documents, and a bibliography, and be printed on the computer with word processing software from the notes students have gathered.

Activities

Activity One

Groups will be formed after students take the Interest Inventory found in Activity Sheet 5-2. These groups should be broad enough to include individual careers within the area of interest. Students should understand that they will be keeping individual notebooks for research that will then be used to create the handbook, and the best of each student's research will be used for the handbook.

Activity Two

Before the groups are formed, discuss and brainstorm with the class what their interests are. Each group should be formed around a broad area of interest, and within each group students can decide on a specific career to research.

Activity Three

Students will prepare for their first interview with an elderly person. Be sure to review and approve the list of interview questions. Working in pairs for this is a good idea because if one student misses something the other can pick up on it. Have the students interview each other for practice and make suggestions for improving their interview techniques before they go on to conduct it. The interviews should be summarized, as should the material gathered from secondary sources. Conduct a class discussion for students to share and summarize the experience of the interviews and what was learned from them.

Activity Four

Again, before the interviews begin, review and approve the list of interview questions each group develops. If you feel that it's necessary, have them do some additional role playing. This activity sheet includes two interviews, the first with someone in the community or from an organization the student contacted for information. This interview should follow the procedure used for the interview with the elderly person. The second is online with experts in the field. Web addresses for this can be found at the end of the chapter. More than one expert should be e-mailed because not everyone will take the time to reply. Explain to the class that the questions in the e-mail messages should be kept to a minimum so as to maximize the possibility of getting a reply. Different questions can be sent to each expert. Again, conduct a class discussion to summarize the experience of the interviews and to compare any e-mail replies they received.

Secondary source material can be found both in print and online. Web addresses are listed at the end of the chapter. The final assignment before putting the handbook together is a comparison of the primary and secondary sources.

ASSESSMENT CHECKLIST

Student's Name _____ Class _____ Date _____

Activity Sheet 5-1   Date Checked _____

> ▸ Did the student:

  ✓ begin to locate resources from local organizations, the yellow pages, or the Chamber of Commerce? YES __ NO __

  ✓ fully understand the assignment? YES __ NO __

  ✓ begin to list titles and authors of print resources? YES __ NO __

  ✓ have a notebook prepared and well-organized to begin the project? YES __ NO __

> ▸ The student is permitted to go on to Activity 5-2. YES __ NO __

> ▸ If the student is not permitted to continue, note the areas of concern and further work that needs to be done.

_____

_____

_____

Activity Sheet 5-2   Date Checked _____

> ▸ Did the student:

  ✓ take part in the class discussion? YES __ NO __

  ✓ write a well-organized composition about the experience that answers all the questions appropriately? YES __ NO __

  ✓ understand that he or she will be researching a career choice within a broad theme? YES __ NO __

  ✓ begin to list careers he or she is interested in? YES __ NO __

> ▸ The student is permitted to go on to Activity 5-3. YES __ NO __

> ▸ If the student is not permitted to continue, note the areas of concern and further work that needs to be done.

_____

_____

_____

Activity Sheet 5-3   Date Checked _____

➤ Did the student:

✓ find an elderly person to interview? YES __ NO __

✓ get written permission to tape the interview? YES __ NO __

✓ prepare for the interview with tape recorder and blank cassettes? YES __ NO __

✓ interview his or her partner and accept suggestions for improvements? YES __ NO __

✓ make notes of the interview and enter them in the proper place in his or her notebook as soon as possible? YES __ NO __

✓ participate in the class discussion and share his or her experience? YES __ NO __

✓ list all secondary sources correctly in the bibliography? YES __ NO __

✓ try to find primary source documents both off- and online? YES __ NO __

✓ completely answer all the questions about these documents? YES __ NO __

➤ Did the final interview indicate that the student followed instructions? YES __ NO __

➤ Were the questions asked relevant to the subject? YES __ NO __

➤ Were all the questions on the activity sheet completely answered? YES __ NO __

➤ Did the comparison between the primary and secondary sources indicate an understanding of the difference between the two? YES __ NO __

➤ Were accurate notes and summaries made from all the relevant information and entered in the proper category in the notebook? YES __ NO __

➤ Did the comparison of resources indicate an understanding of the assignment? YES __ NO __

➤ The student is permitted to go on to Activity 5-4. YES __ NO __

➤ If the student is not permitted to continue, note the areas of concern and further work that needs to be done.

_____

_____

_____

Activity Sheet 5-4   Date Checked _____

➤ Did the student:

✓ contact organizations and find a person to interview? YES __ NO __

✓ follow instructions for interviews given on the previous activity sheet? YES __ NO __

✓ contact several experts online and send e-mail messages with appropriate questions? YES __ NO __

➤ Did the final report from these two interviews include complete, accurate information? YES __ NO __

➠ Were appropriate secondary sources accessed online? YES __ NO __

➠ Were a sufficient number of print sources used? YES __ NO __

➠ Were accurate notes entered into the notebook in the proper category, along with a bibliography? YES __ NO __

➠ Was there a well-thought-out, accurate comparison between the primary and secondary sources that included Web addresses and titles of print materials? YES __ NO __

➠ Did the report about the career choice include complete, accurate information that indicated that the student used appropriate sources? YES __ NO __

➠ Did the comparison between the changes in the workplace indicate an understanding of what changes have taken place and why? YES __ NO __

Final Assessment   Date _____

➠ Did the student:

   ✓ participate meaningfully in all class and group discussions? YES __ NO __
   ✓ maintain a well-organized notebook that contains information from both primary and secondary resources, a completed bibliography, copies of the three interviews, and all the activity sheets complete with answers? YES __ NO __
   ✓ conduct enough research to have fulfilled all parts of the assignment? YES __ NO __

➠ Is the group handbook well organized and complete with a cover, a title, a title page, a table of contents, and a bibliography? YES __ NO __

➠ Is there evidence that the student made a meaningful contribution to the handbook? YES __ NO __

➠ Is an understanding of the assignment evident in the material included? YES __ NO __

➠ Are all the required written assignments complete? YES __ NO __

   • Activity Sheet 5-2: Composition about the activities the student enjoys most.

   • Activity Sheet 5-3: A summary of the interview with the elderly person; a report that includes information about the career as it was in the past, comparing the primary and secondary sources, and includes how the interview differs from the research using secondary sources.

   • Activity Sheet 5-4: A summary of the information from both interviews; a report that gives information about the specific career researched from both primary and secondary sources, compares how this career has changed, and describes how the student believes it may change in the future.

FINAL GRADE _____

   NOTES _____

   _____

ACTIVITY SHEET 5-1
PLANNING YOUR RESEARCH

My father was an egg candler, and even when I was a little girl not too many people were familiar with this term. These days I'm sure no one has any idea that eggs were once inspected for imperfections by candle light. In fact, when my father had this job candles were no longer used. Eggs were inspected with light bulbs, but the name stuck. These days this job is probably done with some sort of technology and people are no longer needed to do it by hand. How many jobs that were once around no longer exist today? And which jobs that we take for granted will no longer exist when you are ready to enter the workforce?

It's important for you to know about the jobs that will be available in the future and to connect with people who are working in those fields and can help you understand the skills and education you'll need to find a career in which you will be happy and successful.

Vocabulary

- ⇥ evolve

- ⇥ primary

- ⇥ secondary

Understanding the Assignment

Each student will take an Interest Inventory and then form groups with students with similar interests. Groups should not be formed based on specific jobs, but rather on the kinds of skills needed for specific jobs. For example, if your interest lies in the sciences and technology, then a group will be formed for that broad area of interest, not a narrow job such as a computer repair person. When you begin your research you will find information about a more specific career.

Using both primary and secondary sources, you're going to find information about how the world of work has evolved over the past several decades and compare the differences between work as it existed in the past and as it exists today, as well as predict changes for the future, comparing the kinds of information you get from these sources.

A pair of students from each group will conduct three interviews:

- ▶ with people who were formerly engaged in work that is similar to the type that interests you.

- ▶ an interview with people who are now working in a field that you want to learn more about.

- ▶ an interview with an expert who is available online to give you information.

All the information you gather will be kept in a notebook that you use only for this purpose and will be used to create a Career Day handbook. When the research is complete each group will select, with your teacher's approval, the material to include in the handbook, such as reports you wrote, any primary source documents, information about how work has changed over the last several years, and information about the specific careers that each student researched. The Career Day handbook should have a cover with a title, a title page, a table of contents organized by category, and a bibliography. If there is an artist in your group, illustrations will make a nice addition.

Be sure to keep all your information in the notebook in separate categories to make organizing the handbook easier. Using who, what, when, and where questions may be helpful.

What Information Do You Need?

Some suggestions follow:

- ▸ What kinds of jobs exist now and will be available in the future that were unheard of even a few years ago?

- ▸ What caused these changes in employment?

- ▸ What kinds of work existed in past years that no longer exist?

- ▸ How is work expected to change during the twenty-first century?

- ▸ What skills and education will be necessary for future jobs?

Where Will You Find the Information?

- ▶ **Library media center**. Print resources such as history books with information about the world of work during the past 60 years, reference books such as *The Occupational Outlook Handbook,* old magazines and newspapers for stories and photos of people at work, autobiographies and biographies of important people in this field.

- ▶ **Interviews**. Elderly people can give you primary source information about their work experience. Interviews with people in the field you are researching will give you information about the present work world.

- ▶ **Internet**. Lots of career information is available online. Your teacher will give you a list of Web sites to search.

- ▶ **Online interviews with experts in the field of your choice**.

- ▶ **The yellow pages of your local phone book**. Listings of businesses and organizations connected with the occupation you are researching.

- ▶ **Chamber of Commerce**.

- ▶ Primary sources such as photographs of workplaces and documents such as pay stubs.

- ▶ Brainstorm with your group to find other resources. If you find something another group might be able to use, let them know about it.

How Your Final Grade Will Be Determined

▶ Participation in all class and group discussions.

▶ A well-organized notebook that contains information from both primary and secondary resources, a completed bibliography, the three interviews, and copies of all the activity sheets complete with answers.

▶ Your contribution to the Career Day handbook.

▶ Required written assignments:

Activity Sheet 5-2: A description of a wonderful work experience you had.

Activity Sheet 5-3: A summary of the interview with the elderly person; a report that includes information about the career as it was in the past, comparing the primary and secondary sources you used to find your information. It should include how the interview differs from the research using secondary sources.

Activity Sheet 5-4: A summary of the information from both interviews; a report that gives information about the specific career you researched from both primary and secondary sources, compares how this career has changed, and explains how you believe it may change in the future.

ACTIVITY SHEET 5-2
WHO AM I?

Everyone has special talents and skills. It's important to be aware of how those talents and abilities can lead to your choosing a satisfying career. Think about the things you like to do in your free time. What activities give you the most pleasure? Do you like to cook, collect things, play an instrument, volunteer in a hospital, paint, build things, or write stories or plays? Have you taken any classes or participated in extracurricular activities after school that you really enjoyed?

Interests and Skills

Discuss your skills and interests in class and then make a list of everything that is mentioned that you are good at and enjoy doing.

Following are some suggestions to get you started. Circle those that interest you.

> ▸▸ What kinds of books do you like to read best?

> ▸▸ Do you like to write plays or stories in your spare time?

> ▸▸ Do you enjoy being outdoors?

> ▸▸ Do you like to work with your hands?

> ▸▸ Do you enjoy being and working with other people?

> ▸▸ Would you rather work alone or with just one other person?

> ▸▸ What school subjects do you like best?

> ▸▸ What are some of the things that worry you the most about the world around you? For example, the homeless, stray animals, incurable diseases?

> ▸▸ Are you very good at using computers?

> ▸▸ What do you like to do best at the computer? Take part in chat rooms or do research?

Continue your list on a separate piece of paper or the back of this sheet.

Tell Us About Your Experiences

Using the list, write a short composition that tells about the activities you enjoy most. Include a really great experience you had while engaging in that activity. Try to explain exactly what it was about the experience that made it special.

➤ Was it the people you were with?

➤ Did it take place someplace special?

➤ Did you try to make something that was really challenging, and the final product came out better than you ever expected?

➤ What did you learn from this experience?

➤ What did you enjoy about it?

What Are Your Career Interests?

Based on your talents and interests, list the jobs you want to find out more about.

Finding People to Interview

You've begun brainstorming in class all the activities that are related to your interests and scanned the want ads to see the job opportunities associated with them. What kinds of clubs, groups, organizations, or agencies might be able to provide information and someone for you to interview?

Using the telephone directory yellow pages, list organizations, businesses, agencies, or volunteer activities where you can find information about those jobs and people who might be willing to be interviewed. Be sure to look under several headings.

With your class, brainstorm all the possible places you might go to find information. Does someone in the class have a relative working at that occupation who would be willing to be interviewed?

Answer These Questions

➤ How do you think some of your skills might be valuable to an employer?

➤ Make a list of five skills that you think would be important in any career.

_____
_____
_____
_____
_____

➤ Which would be the most important to a future employer?

_____

➤ Why is it important to continue learning new skills?

_____
_____

➠ Which of the following do you think are important for many different careers?
  ✓ Oral communication skills
  ✓ Reading and writing well
  ✓ Using computers
  ✓ Working well with others

➠ After the Interest Inventory is complete, circle the group you would like to join.
  ✓ Medicine
  ✓ Law
  ✓ Business
  ✓ Performing and visual arts
  ✓ Science and technology
  ✓ Other

ACTIVITY SHEET 5-3
THE WAY WE WERE

To find information about changes in the workplace you'll need both primary and secondary source material. A primary source is created by people who took part in an event or were at the place when it occurred. Primary sources for this project include interviews with people who have worked in the field you are researching, accessing information online about the kinds of jobs people had in the past, and finding photographs of workplaces and documents such as pay stubs.

Primary Sources

Interview

Working with a partner from your group, you will conduct an interview with an elderly person who held a job similar to the one in which you're interested. These are the people who were actually there, and they are usually very happy to give interviews to students. Relatives and neighbors can be good interview subjects, as can people at senior centers and retirement homes. Be sure to call ahead and make an appointment and explain the kinds of information you are looking for.

Fill in the following information for each interview:

- ▶ Name of person you're interviewing: _____
- ▶ Where the interview will take place: _____
- ▶ Person's telephone number: _____
- ▶ Date and time of appointment: _____

Preparing for the Interview

Practice using the tape recorder before the interview. This would be a good time to interview your partner and to be interviewed by him or her. Play the interviews for the entire group and for your teacher so that they may make suggestions for how to improve them.

Be sure that you have a blank cassette. Test the tape recorder to be sure it's working.

Label the tape with the date and the name of the person you are interviewing.

Set up an appointment with the person being interviewed. Conduct it in a place and at a time most convenient for the interviewee.

Be sure that you have your list of questions and paper and pens with you for writing follow-up questions.

Conducting the Interview

➤ Introduce yourself, giving your name, age, the class, and the school you attend if the interview takes place away from school. Describe the research your group is doing.

➤ Be sure to get written permission to tape record the interview.

➤ Leave the recorder on during the entire interviewing session. You'll be making notes from the tape, and you can't be sure during the interview what may prove useful later on.

➤ Listen carefully while your subject is talking. Often, what a person says may suggest a follow-up question that will produce interesting information. For follow-up, ask who, what, where, why, and how questions.

➤ Try to avoid questions that require only a yes or no answer. Put the questions in a logical order, but be flexible. You may need to ask other questions depending on the answers you get.

➤ If you don't understand something, don't be shy about asking the person to explain it more clearly.

➤ Don't try to rush the interview along. Give people time to ponder and reflect on your questions.

➤ If you need more information, ask if you can come back.

➤ End your interview by thanking your subject. After the interview, send a thank-you letter to the subject.

Some suggested questions follow:

➤ What was the title of the job you held?

➤ What was the highest salary you ever earned?

➤ What kind of education did you need for this job?

➤ Describe a typical day at your job.

➤ How many hours a day did you work?

➤ Did you get paid vacation time?

➤ Did you get other benefits such as health insurance?

➤ Was the job physically demanding or very stressful?

➤ Does this job still exist today? If it does, how has it changed?

➤ Were there any obstacles to women in this job?

➤ What was the most gratifying aspect of your job? What was the worst part?

Brainstorm with your group for additional questions.

After the interview, with your partner or group, listen carefully to the tape several times and make notes of the most important parts. Be sure to enter all the notes into your notebook in the proper place as soon as possible.

» Was there any conflicting information that showed the person did not remember the job too well? Explain.

» What was the most surprising piece of information you found? Why was it surprising?

» What were the questions that led to the most interesting answers?

» Which questions were less useful?

» If it was hard to keep interview subjects on the topic, how did you get the person back to focus on the interview?

» What good follow-up questions did you ask?

» What might have improved the interview?

Each student should write a report about the information gathered from the interview. Be sure to send the interviewee a copy of the final report along with the thank-you note.

Documents and Photographs

You may have relatives who have kept old documents about jobs they held years ago. These may include such things as photographs and pay stubs. You may also find such material in old newspapers and magazines online. Your teacher will give you a list of Web sites to search. Any material you find should be saved in your notebook for the Career Day handbook. If you find material online make a copy, save it, and annotate it.

Answer the following questions:

» Describe any primary source documents you found for this project.

» Where did you find this document?

» What type of document is it?

» What is the date of the document?

» Who created the document?

» Why was the document created?

» What information were you able to glean from this document to use for this project?

» Summarize what you learned from the primary sources.

Secondary Sources

Your secondary sources will be old magazine and newspaper articles from the era you are studying and reference and history books written about the era you are researching. Be sure to list all titles and authors in your notebooks, along with summaries of all the material you found.

Comparing Primary and Secondary Sources

How did the information that you got from the interview differ from the research using secondary sources? Which did you think provided the best information, was more honest, and was more accurate?

Write a report that includes information about the career as it was in the past. Compare the primary and secondary sources you used to find your information. The report should include how the interview differs from the research using secondary sources

ACTIVITY SHEET 5-4
CAREER INFORMATION: THE WAY WE ARE

Just as you used both primary and secondary sources to find information about past work, you'll use both to find information about contemporary careers in the area of work you're interested in. Interviews with an expert online and someone from the community or an organization will provide you with primary source information.

Secondary sources such as reference materials that provide information about current jobs and employment trends for the future and newspaper and magazine articles about the changing work world of today can all be found online and in the library media center. Be on the lookout for magazines that specialize in career information as well as specialized magazines about specific areas of work.

Primary Sources

Just as you interviewed someone for information about work of another time, you and your partner will now conduct two interviews with people who are presently employed in the field. One of these will be online with an expert in the field. Your teacher will give you the Web sites to access. The other interview will be with someone from a community organization, or perhaps a family friend who can provide you with information.

Interview with Person from Community Organization

To conduct the interview with someone from the community, follow the instructions for interviews that you used previously. Fill in the following information for each interview:

- ▶ Name of person you're interviewing: _____
- ▶ Place of work: _____
- ▶ Where the interview takes place: _____
- ▶ Person's telephone number: _____
- ▶ Date and time of appointment: _____
- ▶ Name of organization/company: _____

Interview with Expert Online

The interviews with online experts will be conducted through e-mail. You'll send an e-mail message with your questions to several experts. The replies you receive should be included in your notebook.

▶▶ List the Web sites your teacher gave you to find experts who can help you.

_____
_____
_____

➤ After accessing the sites, list the e-mail addresses of all organizations or agencies you contacted.

_____

_____

_____

➤ List the questions you want to ask each of the experts. Remember, e-mail messages should be kept short and to the point. Show your questions to your teacher to get approval before going online.

_____

_____

_____

Questions for Both Types of Interviews

Possible questions to consider for *both* types of interviews follow:

➤ What skills do I need to develop for the career I am interested in?

➤ Why did you choose this career?

➤ Describe a typical day at your job.

➤ Describe the working conditions of this job.

➤ What training or education is important?

➤ Is there any special equipment used for this job?

➤ What are the most gratifying and challenging things about your work?

➤ Is anything boring about your job?

➤ Is the job physically demanding?

➤ Is it a very stressful job?

➤ What causes stress on this job?

➤ What are the greatest disadvantages and advantages of this job?

➤ Do you use computers in this work?

➤ Do you work alone or with others?

➤ Does your job require travel?

➤ What personality traits make a person happiest in this kind of work?

➤ Do women have to be more efficient, attractive, and harder-working than men in the same field?

» What, if any, obstacles do women face in this field?

» What knowledge and skills are required to do this work?

» Are there many opportunities for women in this field?

» What other jobs can this job lead to?

» What do you think I should be doing now that could help me to get a job in this field in the future?

» Has this job changed since you began working?

» If you were starting over in your career, would you do anything differently?

Write a report that includes the information from both interviews.

Secondary Sources

Look at the table of contents or in the index for specific occupations that interest you. Some of this material will be available in your library media center and online. Your teacher will give you Web sites to access.

Some suggested questions follow. As you do your research, include additional important material.

» How much formal education is needed for this job?

» What skills do I need to develop for this career?

» What are some occupations related to this one?

» Can these skills be transferred to other careers?

» How do the responsibilities of entry-level workers differ from those of experienced workers who hold this job?

» What are the typical earnings of workers in this occupation?

» What is the job outlook in the future for this career?

» What training or education is important?

» What other qualifications are important?

» What changes will occur in this field in the future?

» Will there be a lot of need for people in this field in the future?

Comparing Primary and Secondary Sources

➤ Which do you feel was more accurate and honest?

➤ Did you get information from either type of source that wasn't available from the other?

➤ What kinds of information did you get from the primary sources that you couldn't get from the secondary ones?

➤ Write a report that gives information about the career you researched from secondary sources.

Comparing the Workplace: Then and Now

Write a report that includes the following information:

➤ Why do you think interviews with the elderly are important for understanding the past?

➤ In what important ways are the working conditions of the elderly people you interviewed different from today's workplace?

➤ Are any changes related to technology or to the role of women?

➤ Give evidence for your opinions.

➤ Are there any things that are similar to today's workplace? Explain.

➤ Which jobs that you found out about no longer exist today?

➤ Which jobs that we take for granted do you think will no longer exist when you are ready to enter the workforce?

Be sure to follow your teacher's instructions for entering resources in the bibliography. Enter only those that you actually used. Be sure to include all Web pages in the format your teacher requires.

Career Day Handbook

When the research is complete, each group will select, with your teacher's approval, the material to include in the handbook, such as reports you wrote, any primary source documents, information about how work has changed over the last several years, and information about the specific careers that each student researched. The Career Day handbook should have a cover with a title, a title page, a table of contents organized by category, and a bibliography. If there is an artist in your group, illustrations will make a nice addition.

WEB SITES

Primary Sources

Learning Page of the Library of Congress: Using Primary Sources. © December 1998. Available: http://rs6.loc.gov/ammem/ndlpedu/primary.html. (Accessed October 19, 2000).
Suggestions for using primary sources in the classroom.

Library of Congress. ***WPA Life Histories—Home Page. Manuscripts from the Federal Writers' Project, 1936–1940.*** Updated October 19, 1998. Available: http://lcweb2.loc.gov/ammem/wpaintro/wpahome.html. (Accessed October 19, 2000).
Life histories that include information about occupation, income, and education.

Careers

America's Career InfoNet. n.d. Available: www.acinet.org/acinet/overview.htm. (Accessed October 19, 2000).
Allows for searching by state, resource library, general outlook, and more.

The Bureau of Labor Statistics. ***Employment Projections Home Page.*** Updated September 29, 2000. Available: www.bls.gov/emphome.htm. (Accessed October 19, 2000).
Links to *Occupational Outlook Handbook* and *Occupational Outlook Quarterly.*

Bureau of Labor Statistics. ***Overview of BLS Career Information.*** Updated June 26, 1998. Available: http://stats.bls.gov/k12/html/edu _over.htm. (Accessed October 19, 2000).
Covers "jobs for kids who like" divided by categories such as music/arts and science.

CareerZone. Updated October 11, 2000. Available: www.explore.cornell.edu/. (Accessed October 19, 2000).
Excellent site filled with a wealth of career information.

Exploring Occupations. Updated September 18, 2000. Available: www.explore.cornell.edu/careers/explorin.htm. (Accessed October 19, 2000).
Links to extensive information about many and varied careers. Includes career clusters, teacher's corner, career skills, and much more.

JobStar—Specific Career Information. Updated September 7, 2000. Available: http://jobsmart.org/tools/career/spec-car.htm. (Accessed October 19, 2000).
Pages and pages of information about specific jobs, divided into such categories as health, engineering, retail, science, law, and much, much more, with personal stories from people in the field.

Welcome to FutureScan! Tramp Steamer Media LLC. Updated October 2, 1999. Available: www.futurescan.com/links.html. (Accessed October 19, 2000).
"FutureScans is the first interactive career guide for teenagers." Features excellent information about various careers.

Experts

Ask An Expert. Updated October 7, 2000. Available: www.n-polk.k12.ia.us/Pages/Departments/media/expert.html. (Accessed October 19, 2000).
Lots of links to experts.

AskA + Locator. n.d. Available: www.vrd.org/locator/index.html. (Accessed October 19, 2000).

A database for students, teachers, parents, and other K–12 community members that connects to experts online.

CIESE-Educational Links—Ask-An-Expert. © 1998–2000 Stevens Institute of Technology. Available: http://njnie.dl.stevens-tech.edu/askanexpert.html. (Accessed October 19, 2000).
Long list of links to experts in many fields.

LibrarySpot. **Ask An Expert**. © 1997–2000. StartSpot Mediaworks. Available: www.libraryspot.com/askanexpert.htm. (Accessed October 19, 2000).
Provides links to many sites for finding experts in many areas.

Welcome to Pitsco's Ask An Expert! © 1997–2000. Available: www.askanexpert.com/. (Accessed October 19, 2000).
Lots of experts to e-mail in many categories.

Chapter Six

I LOVE A MYSTERY!

Everyone loves a good mystery, and mystery stories are the perfect vehicle for getting reluctant readers into reading and better readers into reading more difficult books. Mystery stories provide an escape to a place where there is always a solution to a problem and good always triumphs over evil. Youngsters find them exciting and entertaining, and the suspense keeps them alert and challenged as they try to predict the solution to the crime. Fortunately there are good mysteries on a wide range of reading levels available. Many of the short stories of Agatha Christie, Edgar Allan Poe, and Arthur Conan Doyle are appropriate for middle school children to read individually or in class. Radio and television have provided mystery lovers with an endless number of crime-solving characters over the years. Such series as Nancy Drew, The Hardy Boys, and Encyclopedia Brown are still being read, and authors such as Christopher Pike and R. L. Stine continue to write mystery series that are extremely popular with youngsters.

Mystery stories are straightforward and plot driven, with a logical explanation that ties everything together at the end. There is a crime to be solved, clues to be found, evidence to be examined, and finally a solution to the crime. Readers use analytical skills to try to predict the solution to the crime, and the suspense keeps them reading and unable to quit until the very end. These stories are the perfect way to get students to improve their skills as they become engrossed in the plot, setting, and characters and develop a new-found ability that will enable them to move on to other genres.

After students have read some stories in class, they will write group stories using the story elements that they learned about previously. Each group will create a protagonist and a villain and decide on character traits for both. The FBI Web page for youngsters provides loads of great information about crime-solving methods that students can access to develop the way in which their detective will solve the crime. The address appears at the end of the chapter.

Students will maintain individual notebooks and use them to write down their ideas, observations, and experiences that they may use in their stories. They will write preliminary drafts, do peer editing, review, and conference until each group feels that they have the story exactly the way they want it.

All the stories will be put together in an illustrated anthology that will include biographies of all the student authors, describing which of the authors they read inspired their own stories.

After listening to audiotapes of old radio mysteries, such as "The Shadow," students will convert their stories into radio plays, complete with sound effects and music.

PROCEDURE

Materials

Short story anthologies that include a variety of mystery writers, student notebooks, tapes of old radio shows such as "The Shadow," blank audiocassettes, word processing software, photos and music to use as story starters, material for sound effects for the radio play

Equipment

Computer with Internet access, tape recorder

Curriculum Connections

Critical thinking, reading, writing, technology

Objectives

Students will:

▶ read a variety of mystery stories by many different authors.

▶ apply existing knowledge of mystery stories to writing them.

▶ categorize events, settings, and characters in their notebooks.

▶ compare plot, setting, and characters in two stories they read individually.

▶ predict outcomes of stories that are read in class and individually.

▶ understand that reading and writing are interdependent.

▶ explain the sequence of events in mystery stories.

▶ draw conclusions in solving the mystery.

▶ analyze the clues found in the stories to solve the mystery.

▶ evaluate stories written by group members.

▶ collaborate with the group to create an original mystery story.

▶ evaluate each other's stories during peer reviews and conferences.

▶ listen to tapes of old radio mysteries.

▶ create plot, characters, conflict, climax, and a resolution for the story.

▶ use a word processing program to write the story.

▶ create original mystery plays using their stories.

Preparation

Begin the project by discussing mystery stories and explain that after they read several stories in class and individually students will be writing their own group story. Ask the class to name some mystery stories that they have read and what they think makes a really good mystery. Make a list of their favorite mysteries, authors, movies, television programs, and the kinds of things they find suspenseful. Read a few stories aloud in class and discuss the setting, characters, clues, and the crime; list these categories on the chalkboard. The class can try to solve the mystery using critical thinking and problem-solving skills before you reveal the resolution. You might also want to view some television mysteries or movies and have the class discuss them as well.

The stories that you select for reading in class should have an exciting plot, plenty of suspense, and lots of clues that allow youngsters to try to predict the solution to the mystery. Many of the short stories of Agatha Christie, Edgar Allan Poe, and Arthur Conan Doyle are appropriate for middle school children.

Before students begin writing their stories you may want to help them get their creative juices flowing by showing them paintings, photographs, or drawings that you find in magazines or art books. Encourage students to find interesting pictures to bring to class. Have them jot down ideas that come to mind when they view these pictures. Have the class listen to a variety of music. Using a TV hero as a model, or perhaps a newspaper story can be the impetus for their own stories.

Activities

Activity One

Students should learn to be good observers as well as good listeners and should take their notebooks with them wherever they go, keeping track of interesting vocabulary, story plots, and characters and jotting down every idea that pops into their heads. The notebook should be divided into the categories of possible settings, clues, plot, and characters. Periodically review the students' notebooks to make sure they are progressing and writing down their observations.

Activity Two

Students will select two stories to read themselves for analysis, evaluation, and comparison. Your library media center is sure to be well stocked with anthologies from which students can select. The activity sheet should be stapled into the notebooks and the answers to the questions should be recorded on separate sheets of paper in the notebook to make it easier for you to check for completion.

Activity Three

Students will go on to write their own stories using this activity sheet as a guide. It should be emphasized to the class that they should refrain from including any monsters or ghosts in their stories. The stories will depend on suspense derived from imaginative use of clues, plot, setting, and characterizations. Peer review and group evaluation procedures appear on this sheet as well. Students should continue using their notebooks to write down their ideas and observations even after they begin outlining the plot and writing the first draft.

This project is predicated on group stories, with an assignment for each member of a group to write the setting, characters, or part of the plot. The group members should brainstorm each part of the story, but one student can be assigned to write each part. However, if you have students who prefer to write their own stories, they should be encouraged to do so.

The FBI Web page for kids gives lots of information about crime detection methods that students will find helpful. It is included at the end of this chapter.

Peer conferences and reviews are a critical part of the writing process and of this project. After brainstorming within their own group and with you and after the first draft is complete, each group will meet with a partner group to exchange papers and begin reviewing and editing each other's stories. When the story is complete each group will exchange stories with a different group who have yet not read their story to see just how successful each story is. It should be emphasized to the class that partners may offer suggestions for improvement, but only the writers have the right and responsibility to make revisions. Students should be encouraged to share with peers and with you any difficulties they are experiencing. You should also provide time for conferences with you for individual students or the entire group to see how they are progressing as well as for students to ask questions. When all the stories have been completed and evaluated, an anthology will be produced using word processing software.

Activity Four

When all the stories are complete each group will convert their story into a radio play using sound effects and music. If possible, purchase a few old radio tapes so that students can model their own radio show on them. Web sites for this activity are listed at the end of the chapter.

▶▌ ━━━━━━━━━━━━━━━━━━━━━━━━

ASSESSMENT CHECKLIST

Student's Name _____ Class _____ Date _____

Activity Sheet 6-1   Date Checked _____

▸ Did the student:

  ✓ fully understand the assignment? YES __ NO __

  ✓ have a notebook divided into categories for possible settings, clues, plot, and characters and a place for activity sheets? YES __ NO __

  ✓ understand the assessment criteria? YES __ NO __

▸ The student is permitted to go on to Activity 6-2. YES __ NO __

▸ If the student is not permitted to continue, note the areas of concern and further work that needs to be done.

_____

_____

_____

Activity Sheet 6-2   Date Checked _____

▸ Did the student:

  ✓ staple the activity sheet into his or her notebook along with the answers? YES __ NO __

▸ Were separate pages in the notebook used for answers for each story? YES __ NO __

▸ Did the description of the plot, settings, and characters indicate understanding of each?

  ✓ Story One: YES __ NO __

  ✓ Story Two: YES __ NO __

▸ Did the summaries of each story include who, what, where, and when questions to completely describe them?

  ✓ Story One: YES __ NO __

  ✓ Story Two: YES __ NO __

▸ Were all the questions for each evaluation completed?

  ✓ Story One: YES __ NO __

  ✓ Story Two: YES __ NO __

▸ Did the evaluation of each story indicate the student used critical thinking skills?

  ✓ Story One: YES __ NO __

  ✓ Story Two: YES __ NO __

➤ Did the comparison list valid similarities and differences? YES __ NO __

➤ Did the student:

  ✓ use the evaluations for the final summary and make a comparison between the two stories that indicates an understanding of all the elements of a mystery story? YES __ NO __

➤ The student is permitted to go on to Activity 6-3. YES __ NO __

➤ If the student is not permitted to continue, note the areas of concern and further work that needs to be done.

_____

_____

_____

Activity Sheet 6-3   Date Checked _____

➤ Did the student:

  ✓ show evidence in the notebook that he or she has been jotting down ideas for a story? YES __ NO __

  ✓ divide the notebook into categories for settings, characters, and plot? YES __ NO __

  ✓ contribute meaningfully to the group discussion? YES __ NO __

  ✓ begin to write the part of the story that you assigned to him or her? YES __ NO __

  ✓ contribute in a significant way to the first draft of the story? YES __ NO __

➤ During conferences with you, did the student ask meaningful questions and fully comprehend his or her role in writing the story? YES __ NO __

➤ The student is permitted to go on to Activity 6-4. YES __ NO __

➤ If the student is not permitted to continue, note the areas of concern and further work that needs to be done.

_____

_____

_____

Activity Sheet 6-4   Date Checked _____

➤ Did the student:

  ✓ contribute ideas to converting the story into a play? YES __ NO __

  ✓ understand the difference between a story and a play? YES __ NO __

  ✓ fulfill his or her role during the rehearsal? YES __ NO __

  ✓ fulfill the role assigned to him or her during the final taping? YES __ NO __

Final Assessment   Date _____

▸ Did the student:

    ✓ participate in all group and class discussions in a meaningful way? YES __ NO __

    ✓ participate meaningfully in peer review and group evaluation? YES __ NO __

    ✓ complete all the activity sheets? YES __ NO __

    ✓ complete all the following required written reports? YES __ NO __

        • Activity 6-2: Summary of each of the two stories read; evaluation and comparison of the two stories.

        • Activity 6-3: Review of a story written by a different group.

▸ Did the group:

    ✓ work well together? YES __ NO __

▸ Did the final group story include vivid details and descriptions? YES __ NO __

▸ Were the plot and characters well developed? YES __ NO __

▸ Did the story include all the mystery elements as outlined in Activity 6-3? YES __ NO __

▸ Did each group complete the part of the anthology assigned to it? YES __ NO __

▸ Did each student write a biography that included his or her favorite mystery writers, and any authors who influenced the writing done for this assignment? YES __ NO __

▸ Was the final tape a successful rendering of the story, complete with appropriate music and sound effects? YES __ NO __

FINAL GRADE _____

    NOTES _____

    _____

ACTIVITY SHEET 6-1
PLANNING YOUR RESEARCH

Everyone loves a good mystery. They're fun and exciting to read and we all feel pretty clever when we solve the mystery before it's revealed. We also love to watch mystery stories on TV and we all have our favorite detective heroes. But have you ever tried to write a mystery story? For this project you'll not only read some mystery stories but will also try your hand at writing them.

Understanding the Assignment

After reading and listening to stories in class you'll read at least two on your own, describe the plot, characters, and settings, and compare the two stories.

Each group will write a mystery story, complete with a crime, clues, a solution based on the evidence, and lots of suspense. Every student will write part of the story.

As the drafts of the stories are completed, each group will exchange them with a different group, who will offer suggestions for improvement. After changes are made each group will convert their story into a radio play, complete with sound effects and music.

All the stories will be collected in an anthology, complete with author biographies.

Every student will be required to maintain a notebook filled with ideas and observations to use for the story.

Where Will You Find the Information?

Look and listen to everything around you and put all your ideas and observations into a notebook. Keep your notebook divided into sections for characters, plot, and setting. Wherever you are, remember to take your notebook and pens with you to jot down anything that seems useful for a good mystery story. You can always discard unused ideas, or even keep them for a different story.

As you read, make lists of descriptive adjectives and any new or unusual words that relate to setting and characters and can be used for your story.

For ideas to use for your radio play you'll need to go to the Internet, where you can find information about how radio plays are made.

How Your Final Grade Will Be Determined

▶ Participation in all class and group discussions.

▶ Completion of the part of the story that your teacher assigned for you to write, with vivid details, descriptions, plot, and character development.

▶ Inclusion in the story of all the elements of a mystery story.

▶ Completion of the part of the anthology assigned to you.

▶ A biography for the anthology that includes your favorite mystery writers and any authors who influenced the writing you did for this assignment.

▶ A successful rendering of the story on the final tape, complete with appropriate music and sound effects.

▶ Participation in peer review and group evaluation.

▶ Completion of all the activity sheets.

▶ Evidence of participation in writing the radio play.

▶ Completion of the following written assignments:

Activity 6-2: Summary of each of the two stories you read; evaluation and comparison of the two stories.

Activity 6-3: Review of a story written by a different group; a biography to include in the anthology

ACTIVITY SHEET 6-2
READING MYSTERIES

A mystery story must include the crime to be solved, the gathered evidence that solves it, the analysis of the evidence, the identity of the criminal, and a resolution that explains all the events that took place in the story. You've been reading and discussing mystery stories in class. After reading several mystery stories on your own, select two of your favorites and enter the answers to these questions in your notebook. Keep the answers for each book on a separate page and staple a copy of this activity sheet in your notebook.

Vocabulary

➤ analysis

➤ forensic

➤ sequence

▶ **Alibi**. An explanation offered by an accused person asserting that he or she was not at the scene of crime.

▶ **Clue**. Something that appears to give information toward solving the crime.

▶ **Deduction**. Collecting the facts and drawing a possible conclusion.

▶ **Evidence**. Someone or something that proves who committed the crime.

▶ **Red herring**. A false lead that throws the investigator off track.

▶ **Sleuth**. An investigator or detective.

▶ **Suspects**. People who appear to have a motive to have committed the crime.

▶ **Witness**. A person who has personal knowledge about the crime.

✓ ANTHOLOGY: _____

✓ EDITOR: _____

✓ TITLE OF STORY: _____

✓ AUTHOR: _____

Description of the Story

The Plot

➤➤ Write an outline that details the sequence of events.

➤➤ Who is telling the story?

➤➤ What is the mystery that must be solved?

➤➤ What are the most important events in the story?

➤➤ What is the most exciting part of the story?

➤➤ What are the details that keep us in suspense?

➤➤ How would you describe the mood of the story?

➤➤ What are the key clues found in the story that helped solve the mystery?

➤➤ Does the author use any forensic evidence, such as fingerprints, DNA, handwriting analysis, or a lie detector test, to solve the crime, or does he or she use only deduction?

➤➤ How was the crime solved?

➤➤ Were you able to predict the outcome? What clues led you to your prediction?

➤➤ Did the story end the way you expected? Explain.

➤➤ Would you like to change the ending in any way? Why?

➤➤ Change an event in the story that would cause a different resolution.

The Characters

Describe each of the following main characters in this story:

▶ The protagonist.

▶ The antagonist.

▶ Other important characters

Describe the character's participation in the mystery.

➤➤ Does each character speak to the reader, or does the author describe each character for the reader?

➤ Which of the following words would you use to describe each of the characters?

loyal	evil	cold
faithful	tall	short
obese	thin	dependable
genius	master criminal	master sleuth
cooperative	trusted	determined
aloof	diabolical	sinister

➤ If you could be one of the characters, which one would you choose to be? Why?

➤ As you read the story, did you care or worry about any of the characters? Describe that character and how you felt about him or her.

➤ Did you feel that the characters are in a situation that they cannot get out of? Explain.

➤ Would you want to be friends with any of the characters? If so, which one?

The Setting

In a good mystery story it's very important to have a setting that establishes the mood for the story.

➤ Describe the place where this story took place.

➤ Describe the mood that was created. How does the setting help enhance the mood?

➤ What were some words the author used to create suspense?

➤ Was the time of day or night the story took place important? Explain.

Using when, where, who, and what, write a summary of the story, describing the plot, setting, and characters.

Evaluation

➤ Describe what you enjoyed or disliked most about this story.

➤ Do you think the title is a good one for this story?

➤ Can you think of a better title? Explain.

➤ What part of the story did you like best?

➤ Does the action make the story move quickly?

➤ What happened before the story began?

➤ Does the author play fair? Did you feel cheated?

▸ Did the author mislead you by using *red herrings*? How?

▸ Are the clues too easily found?

▸ Did the author use cliff hangers?

▸ Did the opening sentence or first few paragraphs grab your interest? Explain.

▸ Does anything in this story remind you of something that has happened to you? Explain.

▸ Were any parts of the story confusing to you? Explain.

▸ Would you change the ending in any way? Explain.

▸ What do you think might happen after the end of the story?

▸ What part of the story do you feel is most important? Why?

▸ Do any of the characters have qualities that you would like to have? Explain.

▸ Do any of the characters remind you of yourself or someone you know?

▸ Did the author make the setting realistic for this story? How?

▸ Would you ever read anything clse by this author?

Compare and Contrast

Compare the following elements in the two stories you read:

▸ Main characters

What were the similarities and differences between the main characters in each story?

Describe the conflict between the protagonist and the antagonist.

▸ Setting

Are the settings of the stories similar to or different from each other?

Which setting is more suspenseful?

What words did the author use to make it that way?

▸ Red herrings

Describe any that were used in the stories and compare them.

▸ Clues

Describe the evidence that was used in each story to solve the crime.

Were the solutions to the crimes similar to or different from one another?

Using the evaluation you wrote for each, write a short summary explaining which of the two stories you felt was more enjoyable.

ACTIVITY SHEET 6-3
WRITING THE MYSTERY

You've spent time in class looking at pictures, listening to music, watching movies or TV shows, and reading stories to gather ideas for your story. You should have a notebook filled with ideas and observations. Now is the time to share these with your group and begin writing your story.

Your story should not include any monsters or supernatural creatures. The person solving the crime must use his or her wits to find the solution. You can write a locked room story in which a murder victim is discovered in a place without any obvious way out. The detective must figure out how the killer escaped. Or you may want to write a story in which the detective uses scientific crime-fighting methods or deductive powers to solve the crime, or you might want to write a code that must be deciphered before the crime is solved. Your teacher will assign each student in your group to write part of the plot, characters, or setting.

Vocabulary

- ▸ decipher

- ▸ deductive

- ▸ omniscient

- ▸ relevant

The First Draft

This is the time for you and your group to discuss the ideas and thoughts that each of you gathered in your notebooks to begin deciding what to include and how to organize ideas. Remember, you will probably need more than one draft to complete your story.

1. Planning the story. The plot includes the events that happen in the story. A mystery story must include the following:

   ✓ a crime to be solved

   ✓ the evidence and the clues that solve the crime

   ✓ the analysis of the evidence

   ✓ the identity of the criminal

   ✓ a resolution that explains all the events that took place in the story.

   In planning the story, the sequence of the plot should be written down. Know your ending and how you will get there. Some questions for group discussion include:

   Will your story open with a statement about the crime?

   Will the crime be revealed by the detective, the criminal, or a bystander?

   What words will you use to make your characters and setting vivid?

How will you show action building to a final showdown between the detective and the criminal?

What will happen after the crime is solved?

Don't work out the solution too quickly. Build up suspense to get your reader anxious to solve the mystery.

2. The crime. Brainstorm with your group and discuss the things that scare each of you.

   What is the scary situation that the protagonist will be involved in?

   What is the crime to be solved?

3. The evidence or clues.

   What kinds of clues will be available to the protagonist to help solve the crime?

   It's okay to try to fool or mislead your readers with "red herrings," but the readers of your story should know everything the protagonist knows by the end of the story.

   Coincidence is a no-no.

   The solution to the mystery must be logical.

   What are the key clues in the story that will help solve the mystery?

4. Analyzing the evidence

   Will your detective use any forensic evidence, such as, fingerprints, DNA, handwriting analysis, or a lie detector test, to solve the crime, or does he or she use deduction?

   Is there a mystery code involved?

5. The setting

   In a mystery story the setting is very important because it establishes the mood of the story.

   To create a mood you should use your senses to describe the setting and list descriptive words for each place.

   Have you ever visited a place eerie enough to use as your setting?

   Think of a place you've been or part of a movie or TV show that scared you.

Will the story take place at night, during a vacation trip, or just be a day that starts out ordinarily? Describe some feelings you have had, and explain the situation in which they occurred.

   What do the characters *see* at this place?

   If out of doors, is it foggy, sunny, hot, cold, snowing, raining?

   Do they *hear* any strange or unusual noises?

   If the setting is in a city, is there any traffic noise?

   In the country, what noises or sounds would they hear?

   Do they *smell* anything cooking or perhaps perfume, or something they can't quite place?

Do they *taste* anything strange or ordinary?

What do the surroundings feel like to *touch*?

6. The characters. Every once in a while, you pick up a book and can't believe how real the characters seem. There is a good chance the author spent lots of time developing each character. Writing character sketches will help you understand how each character will act, making him or her seem real.

    Brainstorm with your group to create your heroes and villains and find the right words to describe the characters for your story. Discuss what each of you like and dislike about the characters you've read about. Don't copy another author's ideas, but this can give you a way to get started. Characters who fail and make mistakes are more interesting than those who don't. Can you identify with your character? Does he or she seem real?

    The protagonist is the main character or hero. The protagonist must try very hard to catch the criminal. You should make your readers like the protagonist and really care about him or her and the situation.

    The antagonist is the criminal who is trying to keep the hero from succeeding. He or she must try hard to fool the protagonist and escape, or else feel so guilty that he or she confesses. The criminal must appear pretty early in the story, and must stick around and stay in the story.

    To understand your characters, answer these questions about each character in your story. You may not need to answer them all, but select the ones your group feels are relevant to your story:

    What is the character's name?

    Is the character male or female?

    Who are the main characters?

    Where are they when the story begins?

    What has happened to them before the story begins?

    How old is the character?

    Does the character have any siblings?

    If so, what are their ages, and are they brothers or sisters?

    Do they have any pets? Does the character live alone?

    If not, with whom does he or she live?

    Does the character live in a city, a town, or the country?

    Does he or she go to school?

    If not, what kind of job does he or she have?

    Does the character have any hobbies?

    What is his or her favorite food?

    - ✓ Appearance:

        Describe skin color, eyes, height, weight, and any distinguishing physical features such as scars or a limp.

        Does the character wear dark glasses or an eye patch?

        Are the clothes he or she wears neat or sloppy or unusual in any way?

✓ Personality

What things make the character angry, sad, or frightened?

What makes him or her happy or excited?

How does the character react when angry, sad, frightened, upset, happy, or excited?

How does the character look when angry, sad, frightened, upset, happy, or excited?

What is the character's body language when he or she is angry, sad, frightened, upset, happy, or excited?

Does the character have any annoying habits?

What are they?

Does the character make friends easily?

Is the character serious or a cheerful person?

Does the character have a positive or negative outlook on life?

Add anything else you want the reader to know about the character.

7. Dialogue. Remember, the stories will be taped as a radio play. This means that you need to write lots of dialogue.

8. The narrator may take a first person, third person, or an all-knowing (omniscient) point of view.

Who is telling this story or describing the events?

Where is the narrator in relation to the action?

What is the narrator's involvement in the story?

Is the protagonist telling the story as a flashback?

Is the criminal about to commit the "perfect crime?"

Does each character speak to the reader, showing his or her true self, or does the author describe each character directly for the reader?

Whenever your group feels ready, exchange the first draft with a partner group who will review, edit, and discuss ideas and suggestions with you.

Peer Review

Exchanging stories with a partner group will provide you with an audience for trying out your ideas. You may want to exchange stories and have conferences with the other group several times before the story is complete. You will also want to consult with your teacher.

1. Rules to follow:

The writers decide if the story is read silently or aloud by one of the writers or someone from the partner group.

Something positive is ALWAYS stated about at least one thing that was well done.

Listen closely to your partner group's suggestions.

However, the writer always has the right and responsibility to decide to make any changes.

2. Questions for the reviewing group to consider:

    Is the story suspenseful?

    Is the language clear and easy to understand?

    Is the solution too easily worked out?

    Does the story leave out important details?

    Is the ending to the mystery satisfying?

    Make suggestions, but don't be judgmental, and don't get upset if the writers don't follow your suggestions. It's their story!

Your Group Evaluation

At some point during the writing, perhaps after the story is complete, each student individually in your group should answer the following questions. Then discuss the answers with the group and make any necessary changes that everyone agrees with. Your teacher will be the final judge.

▸▸ Are there places where the story wanders away from the plot?

▸▸ What do you think readers of the story might not understand?

▸▸ How will readers react to the different parts?

▸▸ What do you think will be the favorite part?

▸▸ Are the beginning and ending satisfactory? How can they be improved?

▸▸ Do all the clues make sense?

▸▸ Does the solution make sense?

▸▸ Was the reader given all the clues that the detective had?

▸▸ Were enough descriptive words used to make the characters and setting vivid?

▸▸ What words can be added or changed to improve this?

▸▸ Was the solution given away too quickly?

▸▸ Was the situation scary?

▸▸ What is good that can be made better? How can this be done?

▸▸ Is there anything about the story that seems wrong? How can it be corrected?

▸▸ Does anything need to be rewritten?

▸▸ Would it help to try another draft or reread it aloud one more time?

Reading the Story Written by Another Group

When your group story is complete, exchange stories with a group that has never had a chance to read any of your drafts. Answer these questions about that group's story:

- Was the story suspenseful?

- What kept you in suspense?

- Were you able to predict the solution to the crime?

- Did you solve the crime before the ending? How?

- What clues helped you solve the mystery?

- Did you care about the characters?

- Do the characters seem real? Explain.

- Does the story move quickly?

- Did the authors play fair?

- Were you misled?

- Were all the clues needed to solve the mystery present in the story?

Each student should write a review of the story, telling what you liked best and least and what you think could use some improvement.

Creating an Anthology

After all the stories are complete they should be put together into an anthology and kept in the school library. The anthology should include:

- illustrated cover
- table of contents
- title page
- introduction
- dedication
- illustrations
- student biographies

The introduction should include the steps that were taken to write the stories.

Your teacher will assign each group a different part of the anthology. Each student should write his or her own biography that includes information about other stories he or she has written, his or her favorite mystery writers, and the writers who influenced this mystery story.

▶▶| ▬▬▬▬▬▬▬▬▬▬▬▬▬▬▬▬

ACTIVITY SHEET 6-4
CREATING A RADIO PLAY

Your group has now completed the mystery story. It's time to start thinking about converting it into a radio play. You have all the elements of a mystery radio play in your story: a great plot, clues, a brilliant detective, a mastermind criminal, and a setting that's sure to have your listeners scared out of their wits.

If you haven't already done so, listen to some tapes of old radio mysteries, watch a few TV shows and movies, and listen carefully to the music and sounds. Continue to use your notebook to jot down the ideas that pop into your head for using sound effects and music that will help your listener visualize the action, characters, and setting.

Writing the Play

A play is formatted differently than a story. Read a few plays before you start to write your play to understand how to format it and the changes that will have to be made. But don't change the plot, characters, or setting. Use your computer and word processing software to type up the play.

Each member of the group should have a copy of the story, double-spaced and with wide margins to provide room for suggestions. Discuss the ideas that each of you gathered in your notebooks to begin to determine what sound effects and music you'll need, but DON'T CHANGE THE STORY. The sound effects and music the group agrees to use should be noted on each copy of the story.

Keep the point of view that you used for the story. If the story was from the detective's point of view, that should continue in the play as well. You may have to add dialogue. In the story the characters' thoughts were written down, but in a play the listener cannot read the characters' minds. Instead of describing the setting, you'll have to use sound effects and music to set the mood.

Rehearsal

Act out the play, with each group member either playing a character or acting out the sound effects. This is like the first draft of the story, and you should brainstorm and include what works and discard what doesn't. Tape record it. When you're ready, have another group listen and make some suggestions.

Assigning Roles

Everyone in the group will take part in the taping of the play. Depending on the size of the group, some students may need to fulfill more than one role.

1. Actors. Who will play each of the characters and read the dialogue?

2. Sound effects and music. The sound effects people will operate the sounds and music during the taping. How many students do you need to work the sound effects?

3. Prop person. Will be in charge of making sure that everything has been gathered and is in good operating order.

4. Director. Will be in charge of the overall management of the taping.

You already have the most important element of your radio play, a great story. There are four parts to a radio drama: speech, sound effects, music, and silence. Decide exactly what picture you want the listener to imagine in each scene and what combination of the elements you will use to create it.

➤ Will a scene be improved by having music in it?

➤ Will a pause between speeches add to the dramatic effect?

But keep it simple. The story you wrote is the most important element, not the sounds or the music.

Sound Effects

Sound combines with the spoken words in your play to help your audience imagine the scene more vividly and create a picture in the mind of the listener. Sound will make your play seem real. After all, your audience really doesn't know that the cat meowing or dog barking is actually one of you!

Sound effects can be used for such things as setting, showing action, and making your characters more vivid. However, don't overwhelm your play with too many sound effects that take the listener's attention away from the story.

Where to Find Sound Effects

Your library may have recordings of sounds, or you may want to make them yourself by recording and using everyday sounds or by imitating them. You can also find some on the Internet. Your teacher will give you a Web address for this.

Types of Sound Effects

Background sounds and music let your listener know where and when the action is taking place. Will any part of your play take place indoors? How will you indicate the time of day? If it takes place out of doors, how will the listener know that?

Music

You may want to use theme music to introduce and close the play. Background music will create a mood. What kind of mood do you want to create? What music will help create that mood?

Equipment

You will need a tape recorder with a microphone, or a microphone that can be held away from the recorder to minimize noise from the recorder. You will also need lots of blank tapes.

Make a few practice tapes, listen to them, note what should be added, and then when everyone agrees that it's perfect, make a final master using a fresh new tape.

Location

Make your recording in a quiet place. If there is a closet available, that's great. It may be possible for your group to find a place in someone's house or a quiet spot in school for that final taping.

WEB SITES

Crime Detection

FBI. *Kids & Youth Educational Page*. n.d. Available: www.fbi.gov/kids/kids.htm. (Accessed October 19, 2000).
   With a link to the crime detection page that includes fingerprint identification, polygraph, and DNA testing. Also has links to a Junior Special Agent Program, games, and information about working dogs.

Mysteries

Kids Mysteries. *The Case.com for Kids*. © 1995–2000. Available: www.TheCase.com/kids. (Accessed October 19, 2000).
   Mysteries to solve, a listing of TV mysteries for kids, and a writing contest you may want your kids to enter.

MysteryNet.Com. *The Online Mystery Network*. © 1996–2000. Available: www.mysterynet .com. (Accessed October 19, 2000).
   History of the mystery, including Poe, Holmes, Agatha Christie, and more.

Overbooked. *Mystery, Suspense, Thrillers, Crime Fiction*. Established 1994. Available: www .overbooked.org/mystpage.html. (Accessed October 19, 2000).
   Links to all sorts of great mystery book information. Links to mystery sites, organizations, reviews, reading lists, publishers, and bookstores.

Radio Shows

Old Radio Shows Guide. *Old-Time Radio Program Guide*. © 1994–2000. Available: www .old-time.com/toc.html. (Accessed October 19, 2000).
   Lots of information about old radio broadcasts, including where to buy tapes and CDs.

Old Time Radio (OTR) Radio Days: A Soundbite History. n.d. Available: www.otr .com/index.shml. (Accessed October 19, 2000).
   Just click on *Mystery and Private Eyes* to find great information and illustrations.

The Shadow's Inner Sanctum. Updated September 25, 2000. Available: http://redrival .com/theshadow/index.html. (Accessed October 19, 2000).
   Links to everything you ever wanted to know about The Shadow, including a new episode.

Sound Effects

Moviesound: Newton's Apple. n.d. Available: http://ericir.syr.edu/Projects/Newton/12 /Lessons/movisnd.html. (Accessed October 19, 2000).
   Although written with movies in mind, the excellent information is worth a visit. Includes vocabulary, resources, and suggested activities for creating sounds.

Sound Effects for Your Radio Programs. n.d. Available: www.childrensmusic.org/effects .html. (Accessed October 19, 2000).
   Lots of sound effects to download.

Stearns, Jerry. Great Northern Radio Theater. *Radio Sound Effects*. Updated December 22, 1995. Available: www.mtn.org / ~ jstearns/Sound_Effects.html. (Accessed October 19, 2000).
   There's more sophisticated stuff here than you need for this project, but you might want to take a look at it.

 ▶▶| **Chapter Seven**

ART AND THE ENVIRONMENT

In the mid-nineteenth century the artist Thomas Cole founded the Hudson River School, a group of landscape painters whose work often expressed the beauty of the wilderness. Later in the century, as the landscape began to change, many of these artists began painting landscapes that reflected the changes.

Ecological art movements in the 1990s are connected to specific community concerns and are a reaction to the belief that natural resources can be used without any thought to their sustainability. Contemporary artists often work collaboratively with others, such as botanists and urban planners. Accessing *The Getty Museum: Art & Ecology* sites will provide both you and your students with a wealth of information about ecological art. The URLs for the sites appear at the end of the chapter.

Students will be introduced to contemporary ecological art and the Hudson River School of the nineteenth century, focusing on the interaction of society and art. They will compare and contrast the artwork and the historical and cultural context in which each work developed.

Visual art is integrated with social studies, language arts, the environment, and critical-thinking skills, which are enhanced as students use art criticism to analyze, interpret, evaluate, and compare and contrast various artworks.

Students will read local newspaper articles to determine what ecological issues are confronting their community and interview a contemporary artist as well as local officials and members of the community.

Each group will create art focusing on a real community issue based on the information that they gather during research, learning to express their feelings about the world in which they live and to trust their own judgment as they respond to art.

Art journals will be maintained throughout the project and will include examples from magazines, old calendars, and postcards; students' impressions of the art they collect for their journals; and stories they write in response to the artwork.

A display of the art journals and the students' original artwork, with an explanation of the environmental subject and the process used to develop their creations, will be the culminating activity of the project.

PROCEDURE

Materials

Slides of selected paintings; posters, postcards, catalog illustrations, and any reproductions of the paintings available; videotapes, books, and articles about the artists and their works; local newspaper articles about the environmental concerns of the community; encyclopedias and other reference books; word processing software; student journals

Equipment

Computer with Internet access

Curriculum Connections

Art, history, technology, environment, language arts

Objectives

Students will:

▶ understand that art is produced within an historical and cultural context.

▶ apply the theme of the environment to the artwork they produce.

▶ identify local environmental problems.

▶ analyze their own artwork as well as the work of another group.

▶ maintain well-organized art journals.

▶ learn that art can convey a message to the viewer.

▶ describe, analyze, interpret, and evaluate the paintings under study.

▶ compare and contrast the art of different eras.

▶ recognize the works of the selected artists.

▶ compare and contrast two artworks from the Hudson River School.

▶ compare and contrast how and why the art of the different eras has changed because of changing values and conceptions about the environment.

▶ apply what they learned about the art elements and environmental community problems to their group production.

Preparation

Students will study artwork from the Hudson River School and the works of contemporary ecological artists to understand how ideas and values of a particular society and era are expressed through art.

Prepare a bulletin board and decorate your room with posters, prints, postcards, calendars, photographs, material from art magazines, and reproductions depicting the artists and artworks you want the class to study prior to beginning the project to stimulate youngsters' interest. If you have a problem finding reproductions of the selected works, the Internet is filled with excellent sites that you can search prior to beginning this project. The class should discuss the reproductions, and students should write a short paragraph about their impressions of each to read to the class. When the project is complete, show the same slides or reproductions and have the class again write down their reactions.

Explain to the class that works of art often reveal the ideas and values of the era in which the artist lives. Read an excerpt from Walt Whitman's poem "Song of the Broad Axe" aloud to introduce the society in which early American settlers are portrayed as heroes. If at all possible, have someone from a local museum or gallery come in to introduce Hudson River School artists prior to beginning the project. Also, if possible have a local ecological artist visit the class. Try to make a visit to a museum part of this project even if the museum does not exhibit any of the artwork being studied so that students can see the difference between viewing an original painting and a reproduction.

The final project will be artwork that exemplifies the environmental issue of importance to the community.

Activities

Activity One

Each group selects one artist and his or her work from the nineteenth-century Hudson River School and a contemporary ecological artist. Each student within each group chooses a different artwork from the selected artist.

Students will maintain individual art journals, complete with a table of contents, the activity sheets with answers to all the questions, research information about artists and the environment, and their own ideas about their final project as the ideas are developed. Because of the volume of material they will be gathering, it might be helpful to use a word processing program for all written assignments to keep things neatly organized.

Activity Two

Using a variety of encyclopedias and reference books, students answer questions about the conservation movement and compare it with contemporary environmental movements to provide historical and cultural background information.

Activity Three

Students will begin examining Hudson River artists. Each group will choose one artist and each student one painting by that artist. If you cannot find enough examples of the artist's work from reproductions or the Internet, you may want two or more students to research the same artwork, dividing the questions between them. Art criticism criteria are used as students describe, analyze, interpret, and evaluate the painting they have chosen. Use as many of the questions as you feel are necessary, depending on the ability of the students. In the history and culture section are critical thinking questions that require students to do thorough research using a variety of resources. Each student should write a story or poem about the painting and enter it into the art journal in the appropriate section.

Have students choose a partner from another group to compare the works of two different artists. Research into the life of the artist is an important part of the project as well. Many art books can provide this information for these artists, and it shouldn't be difficult to find.

Activity Four

This activity continues art criticism but adds ecological art. These artists may not be as easy to research using print sources, and students will probably need to use the Internet for this. Divide the questions among the students in the group so that they don't get too overwhelmed. If you are lucky enough to get an artist to visit, have the class prepare a list of questions beforehand.

Activity Five

As a final project, students will produce an artwork that depicts how they feel about an important community issue. This can be done as a group or, if you have an individualist among your students who wants to create his or her own artwork, allow that student to do so.

Students will by now have begun to research an environmental issue using local newspaper and magazine articles, as well as interviews with knowledgeable community members, e-mail to local officials, and possibly television. Students should understand the controversy involved. Try to find a guest speaker willing to come to class to discuss the issue. Local politicians are often more than willing to do this. Questions for all the guest speakers should be brainstormed beforehand. After the class has enough information about the issues, each group should begin working on the final production. They should have some preliminary sketches in their journals that can be used. The final product should not be judged on artistic talent but rather on how the student expressed the environmental problem, the effectiveness of the design, and the process used to get there. The artwork should be on display along with the art journals, and parents and community members should be invited to view them.

▶▶ ▬▬▬▬▬▬▬▬▬▬▬▬▬▬▬▬▬▬▬▬▬▬▬▬▬

ASSESSMENT CHECKLIST

Student's Name _____ Class _____ Date _____

Activity Sheet 7-1   Date Checked _____

▶ Did the student:

    ✓ fully understand every part of the assignment? YES __ NO __

    ✓ visit the library and begin to list resources? YES __ NO __

    ✓ start to list people or groups to question about community environmental problems? YES __ NO __

    ✓ understand the importance of finding information in many different sources? YES __ NO __

    ✓ begin to search for illustrations of artworks? YES __ NO __

    ✓ have a journal prepared and well-organized to begin the project? YES __ NO __

    ✓ understand the criteria to be used for determining the final grade? YES __ NO __

▶ Did the group:

    ✓ develop appropriate research questions? YES __ NO __

▶ The student is permitted to go on to Activity 7-2. YES __ NO __

▶ If the student is not permitted to continue, note the areas of concern and further work that needs to be done.

_____

_____

_____

Activity Sheet 7-2   Date Checked _____

▶ Did the student:

    ✓ start the research and begin taking notes? YES __ NO __

▶ Were appropriate resources used? YES __ NO __

▶ Does the bibliography include the titles of books the student has read thus far? YES __ NO __

▶ Were all the questions answered in detail? YES __ NO __

▶ Was the activity sheet, along with the answers, stapled into the journal? YES __ NO __

▶ The student is permitted to go on to Activity 7-3. YES __ NO __

➠ If the student is not permitted to continue, note the areas of concern and further work that needs to be done.

_____

_____

_____

Activity Sheet 7-3   Date Checked _____

➠ Has the group:

✓ selected the artist to research? YES __ NO __

➠ Did the student:

✓ select the painting to use and have an illustration in the journal? YES __ NO __

✓ describe the chosen work accurately in some detail? YES __ NO __

✓ show an understanding of the relationship of the artwork to the historical period in which it was produced? YES __ NO __

✓ select biographies appropriate to the assignment and the research question? YES __ NO __

✓ complete reading the biographical material? YES __ NO __

✓ continue to list the research materials in a bibliography? YES __ NO __

➠ Was evidence provided to support the student's interpretation? YES __ NO __

➠ Was the evaluation well thought out, and did the written work offer a meaningful assessment? YES __ NO __

➠ Was an appropriate, descriptive, fully developed story or poem written? YES __ NO __

➠ Did the comparison of the two paintings indicate that the student had an understanding of both the artwork's elements and the relationship to its culture? YES __ NO __

➠ Are all the questions on the activity sheet fully completed? YES __ NO __

➠ Was everything entered in the journal in the correct category? YES __ NO __

➠ The student is permitted to go on to Activity 7-4. YES __ NO __

➠ If the student is not permitted to continue, note the areas of concern and further work that needs to be done.

_____

_____

_____

Activity Sheet 7-4   Date Checked _____

➤ Has the group:

✓ selected the artist to research? YES __ NO __

➤ Did the student:

✓ have an illustration of the artwork in the journal? YES __ NO __

✓ answer fully all the questions that were assigned, indicating an appropriate under-standing of the work, with evidence to support the interpretation? YES __ NO __

✓ understand the relationship of the artwork to the period in which it was produced? YES __ NO __

✓ identify an artwork from the Hudson River School and a contemporary work, and make simple comparisons? YES __ NO __

✓ find a sufficient number of biographical materials to complete the questions? YES __ NO __

✓ continue to list the research materials in a bibliography? YES __ NO __

✓ participate in class discussion to develop questions for a visiting artist? YES __ NO __

➤ Was the evaluation well thought out, and did the written work offer a meaningful assessment? YES __ NO __

➤ Did the comparison between the two eras include examples of works? YES __ NO __

➤ The student is permitted to go on to Activity 7-5. YES __ NO __

➤ If the student is not permitted to continue, note the areas of concern and further work that needs to be done.

_____

_____

_____

Activity Sheet 7-5   Date Checked _____

➤ Did the student:

✓ participate in developing interview questions for community members? YES __ NO __

✓ participate in interviewing community members and have the names of groups listed in the journal? YES __ NO __

✓ indicate the positions held by any elected officials? YES __ NO __

✓ use appropriate and varied resources to find background information about the problem? YES __ NO __

✓ need to find additional material? YES __ NO __

✓ participate in planning, producing, and evaluating the artwork? YES __ NO __

✓ make a contribution to the artwork that showed appropriate selection of materials, use of art elements, and understanding of the community issue? YES __ NO __

> ✓ indicate exactly what his or her contribution to the artwork was? YES __ NO __
>
> ✓ have preliminary sketches developed in his or her journal? YES __ NO __
>
> ✓ participate in brainstorming and discussion with the group? YES __ NO __
>
> ✓ fulfill the obligation to complete his or her portion of the artwork? YES __ NO __
>
> ✓ show understanding of any controversy? YES __ NO __

➤ Were the results of the interviews accurately described? YES __ NO __

➤ Upon completion of the artwork, was the student able to critique the work with a description, analysis, interpretation, and evaluation? YES __ NO __

➤ Did the group:

> ✓ discuss the environmental issue and agree about the most important one to use for the final production? YES __ NO __
>
> ✓ effectively critique the work of another group? YES __ NO __
>
> ✓ respond intelligently to questions from invited guests? YES __ NO __

➤ Does the finished product fit the purpose the group had in mind? YES __ NO __

➤ Does the finished product reflect the community issue effectively? YES __ NO __

➤ Are the art elements used effectively? YES __ NO __

➤ Does the artwork show an understanding of the community environment problem, and is the design well conceived? YES __ NO __

Final Assessment   Date _____

➤ Participation in class and group discussions was well thought out and indicated an understanding of the topic. YES __ NO __

➤ Appropriate and various resources were used. YES __ NO __

➤ The student displayed an ability to identify and compare the artwork created by artists of both eras. YES __ NO __

➤ The student understands how art changed because of changes in attitude about the environment. YES __ NO __

➤ The art journal is well-organized, with separate categories for each part of the project, and a bibliography. YES __ NO __

➤ All the activity sheets have been stapled in the appropriate place, along with detailed answers to all questions. YES __ NO __

➤ The final project used appropriate subject matter, visual elements, and organization. YES __ NO __

➤ Writing assignments are well-developed and complete with details. YES __ NO __

➤ All the following written reports are complete: YES __ NO __

- Activity 7-3: A report that includes a description, analysis, interpretation, and evaluation of the artwork, and how it represents the society in which it was produced; a story or poem that indicates an understanding of the artwork; a report about the Hudson River artist's life and work.

- Activity 7-4: A report about the ecological artist's life and work.

FINAL GRADE _____

NOTES _____

_____

ACTIVITY SHEET 7-1
PLANNING YOUR RESEARCH

A work of art can be appreciated for its beauty and the skill of the artist who created it as well giving us information about the historical era in which it was created.

In class you have begun viewing art from the Hudson River School and contemporary environmental artists to see how these artists viewed the world around them.

Understanding the Assignment

Each group of students will research an artist from the nineteenth century and a contemporary ecological artist to understand how the artworks of both eras reflect the culture in which they were produced.

The class will find information about an environmental issue that has an impact on the community. It can be a concern about pollution, waste sites, recycling, water, endangered wildlife, or any pertinent concern of your local community. You need to understand as much as possible about why this issue is so important to your community.

Each group will create a collaborative art project based on the facts you found about the community environmental issue and what you learned about the art elements.

Each student will keep an art journal, which should be well organized and include the following categories:

> ▶ Information and illustrations about the artists and their work.

> ▶ The environmental problem your group is researching.

> ▶ A comparison of the conservation movement and present-day environmental concerns.

> ▶ A bibliography of all your resources.

> ▶ Preliminary sketches of ideas for the final group project.

> ▶ All other research, activity sheets, and written assignments.

What Information Do You Need?

Discuss the assignment with your group to make sure that everyone understands it. Consult with your teacher about any concerns you may have.

Brainstorm and discuss with your group what you already know about the artists you're researching, the conservation movement, and local environmental concerns. Be sure to list everything, no matter how insignificant it may seem at the time. You can always get rid of what you don't need later on.

As you do your research, keep writing down all the ideas and questions that you think of and enter them in your journal, placing each subject in a separate category.

Prepare a list of questions to research. Some things to think about follow:

» What was the conservation movement of the late nineteenth century?

» Why was it controversial?

» What led to the environmental movement of recent times?

» Why do so many different people in your community have varying opinions about the environment and feel so strongly about the issue?

Where Will You Find the Information?

Information About Artists

» Use art books and biographies from the school and public library. DO NOT TEAR OUT PAGES FROM ANY ART BOOKS TO USE FOR YOUR ART JOURNAL.

» Pictures for the art journal should come from magazines, ONLY IF YOU HAVE PERMISSION TO CUT THEM OUT.

» Art prints, postcards, and old art catalogs can be used for the journals. Your teacher and librarian will have old magazines for you to use.

» The Internet has loads of information about art and artists. Your teacher will give you a list of Internet Web sites to access.

Information About the Community Issue

» Interviews with officials, members of the community, environmentalists.

» Internet and reference books for background information about this issue.

» Newspapers and magazines articles in local newspapers about the subject. If this is a national or state issue, it will have been written about in other newspapers and magazines also.

» Television. Watch for TV interviews with people on both sides of the issue.

» E-mail to an elected official who is involved with this situation and can give you background information.

Questions for Group and Class Discussion

» List the names of the people and the groups who might be able to provide information.

» What are some of the questions you would want to ask these people?

➤➤ Where do you think the best and most accurate information about this subject will be found?

➤➤ Why is it important for you to find information about the subject from many different places?

➤➤ What problem concerns your community?

➤➤ Where and from whom can you get information about this problem?

How Your Final Grade Will Be Determined

▶ Participation in class and group discussions.

▶ Appropriateness and variety of resources you used.

▶ Your ability to identify and compare the artwork created by artists of both eras.

▶ Your understanding of how art changed because of changes in attitude about the environment.

▶ The completeness of the interviews with local community members.

▶ Your contribution to the planning and creation of the final production.

▶ Your art journal being well-organized, with separate categories for each part of the project, and including a complete, accurate bibliography.

▶ All the activity sheets being stapled in the appropriate place, along with detailed answers to all questions.

▶ Required written assignments:

Activity 7-3: A critical report about the artwork that includes a description, analysis, interpretation, and evaluation, and explains how it represents the society in which it was produced; a story or poem that indicates an understanding of the artwork; a report about the Hudson River artist's life and work.

Activity 7-4: A report about the ecological artist's life and work; evidence of your contribution to the final project.

ACTIVITY SHEET 7-2
THE CONSERVATION MOVEMENT

In 1890 the U.S. Census Bureau announced that all parts of the country had been settled to some degree, and some people at that time worried that increasing urbanization and industrialization would mean the loss of natural resources.

The naturalist John Muir (1838–1914) was one of the strongest supporters of a national park system to set aside land to protect it from development and preserve its resources. He was concerned about what he saw as the importance of preserving the shrinking wilderness. He is often referred to as the "father of the wilderness." In 1916 the National Park Service was organized. Since then many private environmental organizations and government agencies have been established, and many congressional acts such as The Endangered Species Act have been passed.

Vocabulary

➠ urbanization

➠ industrialization

Staple this activity sheet into your journal along with the answers to the following questions.

➠ What is the difference between *conservation* and *preservation*?

➠ Who were the people most responsible for the conservationist movement?

➠ Who were the people responsible for creating the national park system?

➠ List at least three acts of Congress that helped the conservation movement. Give the year they were enacted and what was provided for in each.

➠ Is there a national park in your area? Have you ever visited it?

➠ Have you ever visited any other national park? Write a short paragraph about the experience you had there.

➠ Compare the concerns of the conservationists with the environmentalists of today.

The formation of the national parks was controversial at the time because many powerful businesses were opposed to using land for parks that they wanted for their own purposes. Compare this conflict with present-day conflicts between developers and environmentalists. Give examples.

ACTIVITY SHEET 7-3
LOOKING AT ART:
HUDSON RIVER SCHOOL

The artist Thomas Cole (1801–1848) founded the Hudson River School in the mid-nineteenth century. These painters emphasized the beauty and vastness of the American wilderness while downplaying the harm done to the environment that was brought on by population growth and industrialization. Their paintings often depict an untouched wilderness that was already disappearing.

You have been viewing slides in class from the Hudson River School of art. Each group will select *one artist* from the Hudson River School and each student will select *one painting* from that artist's work. Each group will then compare the artists that they researched with another group.

Enter the answers to the following questions for the painting you selected in your journal, along with the activity sheet.

Art Criticism

Description

Using the reproductions and research results from various sources, provide the following information. Enter your notes in your art journal in the proper category.

▶ Name of the artist your group is researching: _____

▶ Title of the painting you are researching: _____

▶ In what year was this artwork created? _____

▶ What material was used to make this painting? _____

▶ What is the subject of this painting? _____

▶ Describe the place depicted in this painting. _____

↠ Are there people in the painting? If so, what are they doing?

↠ Describe in what way they are like or unlike you.

↠ List all the objects that you see in the artwork.

↠ Which objects seem closer to you? Farther away?

↠ What is the largest or smallest thing you see?

↠ Choose one of the objects in the picture and describe it.

↠ Which object or person is the center of the painting?

↠ What did the artist do to lead our eyes there?

➻ Circle any of the following visual elements that you see:

    ✓ line

    ✓ color

    ✓ shape

    ✓ texture

    ✓ space

➻ List the *shapes* that you see.

➻ List the kinds of *lines* you see and describe them. Are they broken, outlines, curved, straight, wavy?

➻ Where in the picture do these lines appear?

➻ What *colors* did the artist use in this picture?

➻ Which colors are the most outstanding?

➻ How do the colors make you feel? Sad, happy, scared?

➻ What is the *texture* of the picture?

➻ How do you think it would feel if you could touch it? Rough, smooth, hard, soft?

➻ What do you see, feel, hear, smell, and taste when you look at this picture?

➻ Does the painting look friendly? Inviting? Menacing? Sad?

➻ In a few sentences, describe this painting to a person who has never seen it.

Analysis

➻ What questions would you ask the artist about this work if he or she were here?

➻ What visual images are important in the picture?

➻ Why does it stand out? Is it the largest, brightest, or most colorful?

➻ What are the most important or interesting colors, lines, shapes, and textures you see?

➻ Look at all the parts of the artwork, and see how they all work together.

➻ Which element is the most outstanding? Is it the shape, lines, color, or texture?

Interpretation

➤ What other title could you give this painting?

➤ What feelings do you have when looking at this artwork?

➤ Does it seem humorous? Angry? Sad, gloomy, happy, scared, lonely, friendly?

➤ What creates that feeling?

➤ What idea is the artist trying to express?

➤ Does this painting remind you of anything?

➤ Does the work express some experience or feeling you have had, read about, heard of, or seen? Explain.

➤ What do you think is happening in this picture?

➤ What kind of life do you think the people who lived near this scene led?

➤ What evidence supports your interpretation?

➤ Do you think that this painter made this landscape seem more perfect than it really was? Why would an artist do that?

➤ How do you think the artist feels about the subject of the painting?

➤ Do you think there are things in the artwork that represent and are symbols of other things? Explain.

➤ Write a short paragraph that explains what you think this painting is about.

Evaluation

➤ What do you think is good about the painting?

➤ What is not so good?

➤ What do you find most interesting about it?

➤ Would you like to have a copy hanging in your room at home?

➤ Do you think other people should see this work of art? Explain.

➤ What do you think other people would say about this work?

➤ What do you think is worth remembering about this painting?

➤ Do think it is an important artwork? Is this artwork good enough to put in a museum?

➤ What grade would you give the artist for this work? Explain.

➤ Write a short paragraph that explains why you like or dislike this painting.

History and Culture

▶ ARTIST: _____

▶ TITLE: _____

▶ YEAR: _____

Art reflects the time period and society in which it is created.

➤ How does this artwork represent the society in which it was created?

➤ Does it give a distorted view of the society in which it was created?

➤ How can we understand the values of people from other times by looking at art from that period?

➤ Why might people living near this scene now want to own this landscape painting?

➤ Do you think that we in our society interpret this painting differently than people at that time would have?

➤ How does our own experience and culture affect what we see in a work of art and how we interpret it?

➤ Do you believe the artist admired early American settlers who shaped their homes out of the wilderness and that he or she idealized their lifestyle?

➤ Why is it important to know history to interpret the subjects of paintings?

Summarize the information from all the sources you have so far and write a criticism of the artwork that includes a description, analysis, interpretation, and evaluation. Tell how it represents the society in which it was produced.

Choose One of the Following to Write About

Write a short story or poem from the point of view of someone living near this scene at the time it was painted.

Imagine you've stepped into the scene the painting depicts. Write a short story or poem to let us know what you would do and how you would feel if you were part of this picture. What would you experience? What would you be doing? How would you feel? What would you see? If there is a person in the painting, would you talk to the person or run away? Add this story or poem to your journal.

Comparison of Two Artists

Choose a partner FROM A DIFFERENT GROUP. *Each* student must answer these questions, comparing the two paintings that you each studied. Enter the answers in your journal. You and your partner don't need to feel exactly the same way about both paintings, but you do need to explain WHY you feel the way you do.

▶ Name of Artist 1: _____

▶ Name of Artist 2: _____

Compare each of the following characteristics of the two paintings:

▶ The subject of each.

▶ The specific things shown in each picture.

▶ The feelings you get from each.

▶ Describe the senses you would use if you were in each picture: taste, sight, hearing, smell, touch

▶ Compare the art elements in each. Are the lines, shapes, patterns, and colors different or similar?

▶ List the ways in which the two paintings are similar or different.

▶ Compare the outstanding features of each.

▶ Compare how the artists expressed their feelings about the environment in the paintings.

▶ Do you think one of the painters is more critical of the culture than the other?

Information About the Artist

Use your library media center and the Internet to find details about the artist's life. Your teacher will give you Internet Web addresses for finding information about the artist you are researching. Write a report about the artist's life. Include illustrations of artworks in your report. Be sure to include the sources of your information in your bibliography. Include the following in your report:

▶ A timeline of important events in the artist's life.

  ✓ The year the artist was born.

  ✓ Whether the artist is still alive.

  ✓ A description of some historic events that took place during the artist's life that may have influenced him or her.

▶ Where the artist was born.

▶ Several works of art for which this artist is famous.

▶ Any special techniques used by the artist.

▶ The region of the country in which this artist usually worked.

▶ What you might want to know about this artist to help you interpret the works.

▶ The person who had the greatest influence on this person. Was it another artist?

▶ How this artwork might have influenced later artists.

▶ The style of art for which this artist is noted.

▶ A description of any hardships this artist had to overcome before he or she became famous.

▶ Any additional information about this artist that you think is important.

ACTIVITY SHEET 7-4
ECOLOGICAL ARTISTS

Contemporary ecological artists are concerned with exploring community issues and drawing attention to them through their art. Some artists try to increase people's awareness of the need for ecological sustainability. Contemporary ecological artists combine art, ecology, and culture in many different ways, and sometimes work with members of the community such as scientists, landscape architects, and urban planners.

Vocabulary

- ➠ allocate

- ➠ sustainability

Your group will select an artist to research. Each student in your group will be assigned by your teacher to answer some part of the following questions. Use books and the Internet to find the information. Be sure to staple the activity sheet, along with your answers, in your journal.

Art Criticism

Description

- ▶ Artist: _____
- ▶ Title of work: _____
- ▶ Year it was made: _____

➠ What community environmental issue does this artwork address?

➠ Did the artist collaborate with other people? If so, with whom?

➠ What materials were used in making this artwork?

➠ How would the various materials feel if you could touch them? Are they all pleasant? Describe.

➠ Are there people in the artwork? If so, what are they doing?

➠ How would you describe the people? Are they like you or different?

➠ List all the objects that you see in the artwork.

➠ Which objects seem closer to you? Farther away?

➠ Which object or person is the center of the work?

➤ Circle any of the following visual elements in the artwork:

    ✓ line

    ✓ color

    ✓ shape

    ✓ light and dark

    ✓ texture

    ✓ space

➤ Choose one of the objects and describe it.

➤ List the *shapes* that you see.

➤ List the kinds of *lines* you see and describe them. Are they broken, outlines, curved, straight, wavy? Where do these lines appear?

➤ What *colors* did the artist use?

➤ Which colors are the most outstanding?

➤ What is the painting's *texture*?

➤ What is the largest or smallest thing you see?

➤ In a few sentences describe this artwork to a person who could not see it.

Analysis

➤ What questions would you ask the artist about this work if he or she were here?

➤ Look at all the parts of the artwork and see how they all work together.

➤ What are the most important or interesting colors, lines, shapes, and textures you see?

➤ Where does the artist want the viewer's attention drawn to?

➤ What did the artist do to lead our eyes there?

➤ Can you see examples of repetition? Movement? Contrast?

Interpretation

➤ How can the title of this work help you to understand it?

➤ Would you give this artwork a different title? Explain.

➤ What do you think is the most important part of this work?

➤ What do you think the artist was trying to say?

➤ What feelings do you have when looking at this artwork? Angry, sad, happy, scared, lonely, friendly? Any others?

➤ What creates those feelings? Explain

➤ Do you think there are things in the artwork that represent and are symbols of other things? Explain.

➤ What stands out most in the picture? Why does it stand out? Is it the largest, brightest, or most colorful?

➤ What do you think is happening in this artwork?

➤ How do you think the artist feels about this subject? Explain.

➤ Does the work express some experience or feeling you have had, read about, heard of, or seen?

➤ How do you think the painting would feel if you could touch it? Rough, smooth, hard, soft?

➤ Does this artwork remind you of anything?

➤ Would the meaning of this artwork change if the work was produced somewhere else? Explain.

➤ Tell what you think the artwork is about in a few sentences.

➤ What evidence supports your interpretation?

Evaluation

➤ Explain why you like or dislike this artwork.

➤ What do you find most interesting about it?

➤ What do you think is good or not so good about it?

➤ What ideas do you think it expresses?

➤ Would you like to have a copy of it hanging in your room at home?

➤ Do you think other people should see it? Explain.

➤ What do you think other people would say about it?

➤ What do you think is worth remembering about it?

➤ Do think it is an important artwork?

➤ Is this artwork good enough to put in a museum?

➤ What was the artist's purpose in making it?

➤ How successful was the artist in fulfilling his or her purpose?

➤ What grade would you give the artist for this work? Explain.

➤ What will be this work's historical significance for future generations?

Information About the Artist

Use your library media center and the Internet to find information and write a report about the artist whose work you studied. When you finish, be sure to enter the report in your journal. Your teacher will give you Web addresses. Be sure to include the sources of your information in your bibliography. Include the following in your report:

> ▶ A timeline of important events in the artist's life, including the year in which the artist was born.

> ▶ The place where the artist was born.

> ▶ Illustrations of the artist's works.

> ▶ The special techniques used by the artist.

> ▶ The region of the country in which this artist usually works.

> ▶ Names of several works of art for which this artist is famous.

> ▶ Other artists and their work who may have influenced him or her.

> ▶ Whatever else you might want to know about this artist to help you interpret his or her work.

> ▶ A description of any hardships this artist had to overcome before he or she became famous.

> ▶ Any additional information about this artist that you think is important.

Questions About Ecological Art

> ▸ Compare the ways in which Hudson River School artists and the ecological artists express their feelings about the environment. Give examples.

> ▸ If you were an official in your community, what kind of ecological art project would you allocate money for?

> ▸ Do you think that ecological community projects have long-term, lasting effects on the ecological sustainability of a society? Explain.

> ▸ What kinds of environmental issues have been addressed by ecological artists?

> ▸ How does the process of making contemporary ecological art differ from the process of creating traditional art produced in a studio?

> ▸ Add additional information you think is important for this project.

Questions for an Artist

If an artist is coming to your class, work with your group to develop questions. The groups will then discuss the questions in class and prepare a final list. You may want to ask questions about subject matter, materials and techniques, the organization of visual elements, style, and purpose, as well as the artist's life, art experience, and ideas about art.

ACTIVITY SHEET 7-5
EXPLORING A COMMUNITY
ENVIRONMENTAL PROBLEM THROUGH ART

Each group is going to create an artwork that explores a community environmental problem such as pollution, toxic waste sites, or endangered species. Your artwork may take the form of a painting, collaborative mural, collage, or display that tells about the problem and provides a possible solution to it. Be sure to consult with your teacher before starting. Use the preliminary sketches you began to develop in your journals.

The artwork will not be graded on artistic ability but on how well the group shows an understanding of art elements and how well the community issue is expressed.

Information About the Community Issue

Your class has spent some time interviewing members of the community and reading local newspapers and magazines to find information about environmental issues of importance to your community. As you know from studying the conservation movement and the present-day environmental movement, people within a community are not always in agreement about how to act on an environmental issue.

- List the names of the people you interviewed.

- Indicate the positions held by any elected officials.

- What are the results of your interviews?

- Did everyone agree about the most important community issue?

- List the environmental issues of importance to the community.

- Is there a controversy about how any of these issues should be resolved?

- What is the rationale for each view?

- How has your community addressed ecological issues in the past?

- Summarize what action each side wants to take.

- List any additional information you may still need.

- List all the places where you might find this information.

Planning

Brainstorm with your group and, using what you learned about art elements, ecological art, your community's concerns, and your preliminary sketches, begin to plan your artwork. Decide how each group member will contribute to the production of the artwork.

▶ Name of student: _____

▶ Task: _____

▸ What message do you want to communicate through your artwork?

▸ What form will the artwork take?

▸ How will you show your ideas through subject matter, lines, shapes, colors, patterns, and materials?

▸ Is there any artist whose work influenced your ideas about materials and organization?

▸ Be sure to have a reproduction of this artwork and be able to explain how it influenced your work.

Evaluating the Artwork

Write a short critique of your work. Include a description, analysis, interpretation, and evaluation.

▸ Does the finished product fit the purpose the group had in mind? Explain.

▸ Does the finished product reflect the community issue effectively?

▸ Are the art elements used effectively?

Do the same for another group's work.

Displaying the Productions

The completed art journals, with your research about the Hudson River School, nineteenth-century conservation, ecological art, the community issue that influenced your work, and the process used to create it, should be displayed near your artwork.

Be prepared to answer questions from viewers who are invited to come and see the final productions.

Did the display change the opinions of the visitors about the issues represented in your work?

WEB SITES

Getty Museum. *Art & Ecology: Art & the Earth*. © 1999. Available: www.artsednet.getty .edu/ArtsEdNet/Resources/Ecology/Earth /index.html. (Accessed October 20, 2000). "Consists of six photoessays that survey art created to represent the interdependency of people within their environment."

Getty Museum. *Art and Ecology Home Page*. © 1999 J. Paul Getty Trust. Available: www .artsednet.getty.edu/ArtsEdNet/Resources /Ecology/index.htm. (Accessed October 20, 2000).
Covers interdisciplinary approaches to curriculum in art and ecology. Focuses on discipline-based art education and is "both a set of resources for teachers and an online exhibition of contemporary ecological art."

Getty Museum: Art & Ecology Links. © 1997. Available: www.artsednet.getty.edu /ArtsEdNet/Resouces/Ecology/links.html (Accessed October 20, 2000).
An outstanding site and the best available for the study of ecological art, it provides links to ecological artists, artworks, magazines devoted to art and ecology, student-created artwork, museums, and much more.

Hermus Fine Arts. n.d. Available: www.hermus .com/hudson.htm. (Accessed October 20, 2000).
Overview of the Hudson River School and images of a few paintings.

Index of Hudson River School Painters. Updated October 19, 2000. Available: http://dfl .highlands.com/DFL_Painters/Index.html. (Accessed October 20, 2000).
Index to over 1,000 images of paintings. Links to brief biographical information and other museums with additional online images as well as to the Desmond-Fish Library with information about borrowing slides.

Kennedy Center Education Department. *ArtsEdge: The National Arts and Education Information Network*. Updated May 15, 2000. Available: http://artsedge.kennedy-center.org. (Accessed October 20, 2000).
Lots of great stuff!

Library of Congress. *The Evolution of the Conservation Movement, 1850–1920*. Updated October 19, 1998. Available: http://memory .loc.gov/ammem/amrvhtml/conshome.htm. (Accessed October 20, 2000).
"Documents the historical formation and cultural foundation of the movement to conserve and protect America's natural heritage."

The Newington Cropsey Foundation. *Hudson River School*. Updated June 20, 2000. Available: www.newingtoncropsey.com /hudson.htm. (Accessed October 20, 2000). Overview of the Hudson River School of painting and access to thousands of online images.

Pacific Bell. *EYES on Art*. © 1998–2000; updated October 1, 1998. Available: www.kn.pacbell .com/wired/art2/. (Accessed October 20, 2000).
Although not updated for awhile, still a really nice way for students to learn about looking at art. With a teacher's guide, images for study, questions about each, and much more.

 ▶▶▎ **Chapter Eight**

IT TAKES ALL KINDS: LEARNING ABOUT BIOMES

Extinction is nothing new. Species that have not been able to adapt have been disappearing for millions of years. However, humans are hastening the speed with which extinction is taking place by plundering nature's gifts as well as through the growth of human populations. Students need to be aware of the diversity of species found on Earth, why it's important to conserve these species, how they can help slow the negative impact of human intervention, and the consequences to the future if the destruction is not halted.

This chapter focuses on the diversity of species found in the land biomes of the United States. Biomes can be defined by a number of specific characteristics, including a unique climate and a population of specific animal and plant species.

Students will identify the locations of the biomes in the United States, learn what makes each of these places unique, and discover the relationship between the people who live there and the natural environment. They will become aware of the effects humans have on the environment, both beneficial and harmful, and will learn how people have altered the environment to better suit their needs, as well as the consequences of many of these actions on the natural environment.

The geographic themes of location, place, region, and the relationship of people to the natural environment will be emphasized and will be integrated with social studies, technology, and language arts. Students will research the endangered species found in the biome their group is studying, becoming knowledgeable about how conservation can help limit the destruction of the natural world.

Students will maintain individual journals, divided into categories of information, which will later be used for creating a database of all the information they gathered throughout the project.

As information technology plays a bigger role in society, the ability to organize data and think critically about them is becoming essential for success in work. Our day-to-day lives interact more and more with databases in some form or other, whether as daily attendance reports, supermarket purchases, or video rentals. Earning a living and running our lives increasingly depends on how we use databases to find and maximize important information.

155

PROCEDURE

Materials

Maps and atlases of the United States; newspapers and magazine articles about endangered species; print, CD-ROM, and online encyclopedias; animal encyclopedias, reference books with illustrations of world regions and plant and animal species; database software such as ClarisWorks or Microsoft Works; student journals; recordings of songs by Pete Seeger, Paul Winter, and John Denver

Equipment

Computer with Internet and e-mail access

Curriculum Connections

Language arts, science, geography, social studies

Objectives

Students will:

► use map skills to locate the biome being researched.

► use longitude and latitude to locate areas within the biome.

► identify biomes and the physical characteristics and species of each.

► understand how geographic location affects such things as vegetation and soil.

► create a map of the biome they are researching.

► compare and contrast the characteristics of the biomes.

► identify indigenous plants and animals from each of the biomes.

► identify threats to the habitat of the biomes in the United States.

► evaluate the effects of changes that people make to the natural environment.

► describe the impact humans have on various species.

► explain how human survival needs affect the environment.

► examine different points of view regarding the use of the environment.

► identify a variety of both print and nonprint reference materials.

► use computer skills to e-mail local and national lawmakers.

► create a journal of all the information gathered.

► create a database that compares the biomes.

Preparation

Create a bulletin board with pictures of the various biomes, a map of the United States, and recent magazine and newspaper articles about endangered species. Start with a discussion of the physical characteristics and the climate of your area and compare these characteristics with other areas of the country that your students may have visited. They may have friends and relatives in these regions who can provide information and pictures. Brainstorm the factors that make these places distinct from each other. Explain that scientists have many ways of classifying biomes, but this project is investigating only the land biomes of the United States. Students should discuss the importance of biodiversity and understand how we are interconnected with the natural world. Discuss some of the reasons why human beings take over natural areas and how preserving natural habitats might also support human needs.

Each group will select a biome located in the United States to research and investigate its species, the conditions under which the species live, any endangered species found in the area, why they are endangered, why we should be concerned about this, and what, if anything, can be done to prevent extinction of the species.

Students will maintain journals that include the completed activity sheets, all the research notes, any poems or stories, and illustrations and maps, as well as newspaper and magazine articles related to the location they are studying and anything relevant that the students wish to include. For extra credit students can create a collage of pictures of the species found in the biomes.

Activities

Activity One

Groups should be formed after the students understand the assignment and class discussion is underway. A list of criteria for grading the assignment is included here.

Activity Two

This activity introduces map skills. Students will find the location of the biome they are researching and answer the questions about latitude, scale, and legends. If your students are familiar with using maps, you may want to use this activity sheet for review. Each group will make maps of the biome they are studying. Each student selects a different area or a different kind of map and includes locations for some of the sites, a legend, and a scale. Students should get your approval of what they intend to do before starting.

Activity Three

This activity provides questions for each of the biomes and is pretty straightforward, providing background information for the project. The answers can easily be found in print encyclopedias, atlases, and online. You may want to assign specific questions to each student in the group. Students should begin putting the information into categories in their journals.

Activity Four

The questions in this activity require critical thinking skills as students use the information to understand how these regions have changed because of human intervention, the risks that still exist, and what, if anything, can be done to alleviate the problems. There are two writing assignments to be completed. The first summarizes the information gathered describing the biome that was researched. The second requires each student to find information about government or other agencies concerned with the issue of endangered species. These organizations all have Web pages, some of which are listed at the end of the chapter. If you have e-mail access, each student should send a message to these organizations for further information. There are questions provided for class discussion.

Activity Five

All the information that has been categorized in the journal will now be used to create a database. Explain to the class before they begin just what a database is and try to have an example of one on hand before they begin this activity. The information in this activity sheet is for the simplest form of database. Depending on your class's experience and ability, you may want to get a little more sophisticated.

ASSESSMENT CHECKLIST

Student's Name _____ Class _____ Date _____

Activity Sheet 8-1   Date Checked _____

➤ Did the student:

   ✓ fully understand the assignment? YES __ NO __

   ✓ develop appropriate research questions? YES __ NO __

   ✓ begin to list print resources? YES __ NO __

   ✓ prepare a journal with different areas for categories to begin the project? YES __ NO __

➤ The student is permitted to go on to Activity 8-2. YES __ NO __

➤ If the student is not permitted to continue, note the areas of concern and further work that needs to be done.

_____

_____

_____

Activity Sheet 8-2   Date Checked _____

➤ Did the student:

   ✓ completely answer all the questions about direction, location, scale, and legends? YES __ NO __

   ✓ create a map that included topographic features, a legend, and locations of various places found in the biome? YES __ NO __

➤ The student is permitted to go on to Activity 8-3. YES __ NO __

➤ If the student is not permitted to continue, note the areas of concern and further work that needs to be done.

_____

_____

_____

Activity Sheet 8-3   Date Checked _____

➤ Did the student:

   ✓ answer all the assigned questions in detail? YES __ NO __

   ✓ select appropriate reference materials to complete the assignment and the research questions? YES __ NO __

   ✓ continue to list the research materials in a bibliography? YES __ NO __

✓ put the complete, detailed information in the proper category in the journal? YES __ NO __

▸▸ The student is permitted to go on to Activity 8-4. YES __ NO __

▸▸ If the student is not permitted to continue, note the areas of concern and further work that needs to be done.

_____

_____

_____

Activity Sheet 8-4   Date Checked _____

▸▸ Did the student:

✓ give detailed, thoughtful answers to the questions that indicated an understanding of the subject, and provide evidence when called for? YES __ NO __

✓ contribute to the group and class discussions? YES __ NO __

✓ complete an essay about the biome that provided complete, detailed information and indicated a thorough understanding of the subject? YES __ NO __

✓ access the organization's Web site to find needed information? YES __ NO __

✓ send an e-mail message to the agency for further information? YES __ NO __

✓ complete a second report using the information from the organization that showed insight and understanding of the problem? YES __ NO __

▸▸ The student is permitted to go on to Activity 8-5. YES __ NO __

▸▸ If the student is not permitted to continue, note the areas of concern and further work that needs to be done.

_____

_____

_____

Activity Sheet 8-5   Date Checked _____

▸▸ Did the student:

✓ participate in both group and class discussion concerning creating and evaluating the database? YES __ NO __

✓ make suggestions for improving the database? YES __ NO __

Final Assessment   Date _____

▸▸ Did the group:

✓ locate a sufficient number of maps to give each student the needed information? YES __ NO __

➤ Did the student:

    ✓ create a final version of his or her map of the biome that included all the necessary features? YES __ NO __

    ✓ participate in and contribute to all group and class discussions? YES __ NO __

    ✓ make meaningful contributions to the database that included all the necessary features called for on the activity sheet? YES __ NO __

    ✓ divide the journal into categories and include copies of all activity sheets with completed answers, summarized articles from newspapers and magazines, illustrations, poems or stories, and a bibliography? YES __ NO __

    ✓ complete the following required written reports, indicating an understanding of the issue: YES __ NO __

- A description of the biome the student researched, illustrated with pictures of the plant and animal life, including information about its location, climate, unique features, and how humans may have adversely affected its environment.

- A report about the agency or organization involved in wildlife protection that includes information asked for in Activity 8-4, and indicating that the student used critical thinking in answering the questions.

FINAL GRADE _____

    NOTES _____

_____

▶▶

ACTIVITY SHEET 8-1
PLANNING YOUR RESEARCH

Scientists classify the regions of the Earth into biomes according to the climate, soil, and the animal and plant species found in the region. These biomes may be found quite far from one another. For example, all the deserts of the world represent a single biome, although there are deserts in many places.

Human beings could not exist without the riches and diversity of all the plants, animals, and micro-organisms found in the many diverse places on Earth. We depend on these species for our food, medicines, and many everyday products. The greater the variety of species, the greater the number of resources that are available to us.

Vocabulary

▸▸ species

▸▸ topography

Understanding the Assignment

To begin the assignment, each group of students will select a land biome found in the United States to research. Each group will explore the characteristics of the biome they are researching and describe the species found in the region, the risks to its environment, and the impact humans have had on the natural life of the region.

The class will create a database that contrasts the biomes and their endangered species.

Each student will be responsible for maintaining a journal, divided into categories that will be used for the database. The journal should include copies of all activity sheets and completed answers, summarized articles from newspapers and magazines, illustrations, any poems or stories you write or find about endangered species, and a bibliography of all the resources in which you found information.

What Information Do You Need?

Brainstorm with your group and develop at least three questions that will help you find your information. Some suggestions follow:

▸▸ What is being done to preserve habitats in the United States?

▸▸ How can students help?

▸▸ Why is this a controversial topic?

Where Will You Get the Information?

▶ **Encyclopedias**

Print, CD-ROM, and online encyclopedias. Background information about your topic.

Animal encyclopedias. Pictures and loads of information about the animals.

▶ **Atlases.** Many different types of maps of the regions you're studying and additional information.

▶ **Professional organizations and government agencies.** Your teacher will give you the Web page URLs she wants each student to access.

▶ **Newspapers and magazines.** It seems that there is an article almost every day about endangered species. Be on the lookout for these; read, summarize, and keep them in your journals.

▶ **Literature and music.** Can you find stories or poems about endangered species? Do you know the songs of Pete Seeger, John Denver, and others who wrote about this topic?

▶ Other resources that you and the other students in your group think of.

How Your Final Grade Will Be Determined

▶ A journal complete with copies of all activity sheets and completed answers, summarized articles from newspapers and magazines, illustrations, any poems or stories you write or find about endangered species, and a bibliography of all the resources in which you found information.

▶ Participation in class and group discussions.

▶ A map that includes all the required features.

▶ Having made meaningful suggestions and contributions for creating and evaluating the database.

▶ Required written assignments:

A description of the biome your group researched, illustrated with pictures of the plant and animal life, that includes information about its location, climate, unique features, and the way in which humans may have adversely affected its environment.

A report that describes the work of a government agency or organization involved in wildlife protection.

ACTIVITY SHEET 8-2
USING MAPS TO LOCATE THE BIOMES
OF THE UNITED STATES

Your class has been discussing the biomes and the diversity of species found in different areas of the United States. Scientists have many different ways of classifying them. For this project each group has selected one of the following biomes to research: tundra, coniferous forest, temperate deciduous forest, grassland, desert, rain forest, or chaparral.

Maps are made for a variety of purposes, and there can be many maps of the same place that emphasize different features of a particular location. Because it's impossible to put all the information about a place on one map, you may need to look at several different maps to find your information.

Vocabulary

- adaptation
- coniferous
- temperate
- deciduous

Kinds of Maps

- **Topographic map**. Gives a description of the physical features of a location.
- **Road map**. Shows people how they can travel from one place to another. Also shows some physical boundaries, such as mountains and rivers.
- **Political map**. Shows boundaries between states, counties, cities, towns, and villages.

What other kinds of maps can you think of?

Finding the Biome

Circle the biome your group is researching.

- tundra
- coniferous forest
- temperate deciduous forest
- grassland
- desert
- chaparral
- rain forest

Direction

In addition to using north, south, east, and west to describe direction, northeast, southeast, southwest, and northwest are also used to determine direction.

In which part of the country is this biome found? In which state or states?

Select two large cities located in the biome. In what direction would you travel to get from one to the other?

In your biome, which town or city is farthest south? Which towns are farthest east? Which towns are farthest west?

Longitude and Latitude

These imaginary lines allow us to find the location of any place on the globe or map:

> ▶ **Latitude** tells us how far north or south of the equator a place is. How does the latitude of the biome you are researching affect the climate?

> ▶ **Longitude** measures distance east and west of the prime meridian.

> ▶ The **prime meridian** is an imaginary line running between the North Pole and the South Pole through Greenwich, England.

➨ What is the location of a national park found in the biome?

➨ Find the location of the two largest cities. What is their latitude?

➨ Find a body of water in the biome and give its location.

➨ Using a globe, pick a city in the biome and follow its latitude line around the globe. Find two or three other cities located at about the same latitude.

Scale

The relationship between a distance on the map and the distance on the ground is known as *scale*. One reason many people use maps is to determine the distance between two places. Each map has its own distance scale printed on it. Large-scale maps show a small land area in great detail. Small-scale maps show less detail but a larger land area. What is the scale of the map you are using? Select two points on the map and use your ruler to measure the distance between the two.

Legends

Legends explain the symbols that appear on a map. Every map's legend is different.

➨ What are the major colors on the map you are using?

➨ What does each color represent?

➤➤ What color is used for bodies of water?

➤➤ What symbol is used for mountains?

➤➤ Use the legend to find the symbol for airports.

➤➤ What symbol is used for state capitals? Find a state capital on your map.

Making a Map

Each student in your group will draw a map of the biome that describes its various features. How will you as a mapmaker decide what information is needed?

➤➤ Will you draw a physical, political, highway, or weather map?

➤➤ Be sure to show all the topographic features on your map.

➤➤ You will need to devise a legend for your map.

➤➤ What symbols will you use for mountains, highways, lakes, rivers, forests, cities?

➤➤ Be sure to indicate the latitude of various places.

➤➤ How does the location affect the climate?

ACTIVITY SHEET 8-3
DESCRIPTION OF THE BIOMES

Only certain species are naturally found in any particular place. For example, a cactus is found in the desert, and polar bears are only found in the Arctic. Plants and animals live in ecological communities and are adapted to the same living conditions so that they can all live in the same place.

Vocabulary

⇥ adaptation	⇥ carnivore
⇥ ecotone	⇥ herbivore
⇥ indigenous	⇥ reconcile
⇥ replenish	⇥ riparian
⇥ topography	⇥ urbanization

Answer the following questions *only for the biome* your group is researching. Divide the questions among the students in your group. Put the answers into the proper category in your journal.

Chaparral

▶ Location:

   In which part of the United States is this biome located?

   In which states?

▶ Climate:

   Describe the climate of this biome.

   What is the average annual rainfall?

   What weather disasters are prevalent in this part of the country?

   What conditions cause them?

▶ Animal life:

   Describe two animals that are indigenous to this biome.

   Describe their habitats, diet, and survival skills.

   List any animals found here that are endangered.

▶ Plant life:

   Describe the kinds of plants found here.

   Describe how plants have adapted to the various weather conditions.

List any plants found here that are endangered.

List any plants that were once found here and are now extinct.

▶ Unique features:

What are the characteristics of climate, soil, vegetation, and topography that make this biome special and different from other places?

▶ Additional information:

What other interesting facts have you found about this biome?

List any animals that were once found here and are now extinct.

What were they used for?

What led to their becoming extinct?

Temperate Grasslands

This biome is found on many continents, and each is designated by a different name.

➨ By what name is this biome known in the United States?

➨ By what name is this biome known in South America?

➨ By what name is this biome known in South Africa?

▶ Location:

In what part of the United States is this biome located?

Name the states that are located in this biome.

▶ Climate:

Describe the climate and the annual rainfall.

What are the growing seasons of the biome?

What products are grown here?

▶ Animal life:

Describe two animals that are indigenous to this biome.

Describe their habitats, diet, and survival skills.

Describe some birds found in this biome.

List any species found here that are endangered.

▶ Plant life:

Describe the indigenous plants of this region.

What plants once thrived on the prairies that are now extinct?

The flowers found in this region are unusual. Describe some of them and illustrate.

How do the plants help the animals?

Name some of the grasses that grow in this region.

▶ Unique features:

What are the characteristics of climate, soil, vegetation, and topography that make this biome special and different from other places?

▶ Additional information:

What other interesting facts have you found about this biome?

Rain Forest

▶ Location:

Where in the United States is the rain forest located?

▶ Climate:

Describe the climate.

How are the rain forests important to the world's climate?

▶ Animal life:

Describe some of the indigenous animals found in this region.

Name some of the endangered species of this biome.

Describe their habitats, diet, and survival skills.

Describe some of the reptiles and birds of this biome.

▶ Plant life:

How does the climate affect the growth of trees and flowers?

Why is it important not to destroy the many species found here?

▶ Unique features:

What are the characteristics of climate, soil, vegetation, and topography that make this biome special and different from other places?

What features make the rain forest unique?

How does science use these many species of the rain forest?

▶ Additional information:

What other interesting facts have you found about this biome?

List any animals that were once found here and are now extinct.

What were they used for?

What led to their becoming extinct?

Coniferous Forest (Taiga)

▶ Location:

In what part of the United States is this biome located?

In which states is this biome located?

▶ Climate:

Describe the climate of this region.

Describe the seasons.

What is the annual rainfall?

What is the average daily temperature?

▶ Animal life:

Name the indigenous animals of this region.

Describe their habitats, diet, and survival skills.

List some of the endangered animals in this area.

▶ Plant life:

Describe some of the trees of this biome and illustrate them.

How do the trees help animal life?

▶ Unique features:

Name some rivers in this region.

What fish are found here?

What are humans doing to help destroy this population?

What can be done to help these fish survive?

What are the characteristics of climate, soil, vegetation, and topography that make this biome special and different from other places?

▶ Additional information:

What other interesting facts have you found about this biome?

List any animals that were once found here and are now extinct.

What were they used for?

What led to their becoming extinct?

Temperate Deciduous Forest

▶ Location:

In what part of the country is this biome found?

In which states?

▶ Climate:

Describe the climate of this region.

Describe the seasons.

What is the annual rainfall?

How is the climate unique?

▶ Animal life:

    Describe some of the indigenous animals and birds of this region

    How have they adapted to survive under the climatic conditions found here?

    Describe their habitats, diet, and survival skills.

    List some of the endangered animals in this area.

▶ Plant life:

    Describe some of the common plants and illustrate them.

    Describe some of the trees found in this area and illustrate them.

▶ Unique features:

    What are the characteristics of climate, soil, vegetation, and topography that make this biome special and different from other places?

▶ Additional information:

    What other interesting facts have you found about this biome?

    List any animals that were once found here and are now extinct.

    What were they used for?

    What led to their becoming extinct?

Desert

▶ Location:

    List the names of the deserts and the states in which they are located.

    In which part of the country are they found?

▶ Climate:

    Describe the climate of the desert.

    What is the annual rainfall?

    How does the climate of the desert differ from other biomes?

▶ Animal life:

    Describe the indigenous animals, reptiles, and amphibians found here.

    How do animals survive in this climate?

    List any endangered animals.

    How has introducing non-native species affected the area?

▶ Plant life:

    How have plants adapted to the climate?

    How are grasses that were introduced some time ago affecting the native species?

    Why were these plants brought into the desert?

List any endangered species of plants.

Are any that once grew here now extinct?

▶ Unique features:

What are the characteristics of climate, soil, vegetation, and topography that make this biome special and different from other places?

▶ Additional information:

What other interesting facts have you found about this biome?

List any animals that were once found here and are now extinct.

What were they used for?

What led to their becoming extinct?

Tundra

▶ Location:

Where in the United States is this biome located?

In which state?

▶ Climate:

Describe the climate of this biome.

What is the average temperature?

What is unique about the seasons in this region?

What is permafrost?

▶ Animal life:

Describe some of the animals and birds found in this region.

How have animals adapted?

Describe their hibernation patterns.

▶ Plant life:

How have plants adapted to the climate?

▶ Unique features:

What are the characteristics of climate, soil, vegetation, and topography that make this biome special and different from other places?

▶ Additional information:

What other interesting facts have you found about this biome?

List any animals that were once found here and are now extinct.

What were they used for?

What led to their becoming extinct?

ACTIVITY SHEET 8-4
ENDANGERED SPECIES

An endangered species is one that is in immediate danger of becoming extinct. *Extinction,* which has occurred throughout time, happens when an animal is unable to adapt to its changing environment. It's happening much faster now than at any other time in the planet's history. As human populations grow, people use more land, and species and their habitats disappear.

Biodiversity describes the variety of life on Earth. Many of the huge variety of plants and animals found on Earth are used for medicine, food, and everyday products. New species are still being discovered, and we don't know which of these may some day be the answer to many diseases prevalent in the world. However, when a species becomes extinct it may happen before we have the chance to explore its possible benefits. Because so many species depend on other species, one extinction can lead to many more, threatening future discoveries. No one knows how many millions of species exist, but unfortunately many species, both known and unknown to science, are now being lost forever.

Vocabulary

- adverse
- degradation
- extinct
- predator
- sanctuary
- deforestation
- endangered
- habitat
- prey
- threatened

Answer these questions *only for the biome* your group is researching. Your teacher will divide the questions among the students in your group.

History

- What kinds of animals lived in the biome in the past?
- How were they important during the development of the region?
- How were these animals used?
- Were there any plant species that are now extinct?
- What caused these species to become extinct?

Endangered Species

➠ List the endangered species found in the biome your group is researching.

➠ Where in the biome are these species found?

➠ Why is it important to protect these species?

➠ Are there any introduced species of animals or plants?

➠ Have they affected the environment of the area you are studying? Explain.

Human Impact

Every group answers these questions.

➠ What risk factors affect this biome?

➠ How are these plants and animals threatened by human activity?

➠ How do the unique characteristics of this region affect the people living there?

➠ In what ways have the people who live in this area adjusted to their environment?

➠ How has the habitat been changed or lost as a consequence of human activity?

➠ Has any human activity already destroyed any of the species that were once prevalent in this area?

➠ Are these activities important for human survival?

➠ Is it possible to balance the animals' needs against human needs? How would you do this?

➠ What jobs in the area are dependent on a healthy environment?

➠ Which jobs are lost because of habitat degradation?

➠ If the environment is permanently changed or damaged, how might that affect the future?

➠ What causes pollution in this area?

➠ What is the effect of this pollution?

Rain Forest Only

➠ What is meant by "slash and burn?"

➠ Can the rain forest be replenished? Explain.

➠ Why is it important not to destroy the many species found here?

» What industry helps destroy the forest?

» Are these products necessary for human survival?

» What can be done to reconcile the needs of the forest with the needs of humans?

» What can be done to stop this destruction of the forest?

» Why is it important to conserve forests?

» What effect does forest destruction have on global climate?

Deciduous Forest Only

The deciduous forest is very different now than what it was when the first settlers arrived.

» During what period of this country's development was a great deal of the land cleared? For what purpose?

» Describe some of the pollutants that damaged the environment of this region.

» What is being done to stop this pollution?

» Why is it important for humans to maintain forests?

» What can be done now to conserve the trees that were previously lost?

Desert Only

» What are riparian habitats?

» How were they destroyed?

» How has urbanization affected deserts?

» What is desertification?

» What factors lead to this?

» What are the consequences?

» What industries have contributed to these problems?

» Are these industries necessary for human survival? Explain.

Protecting Species

Every group answers these questions. Wildlife refuges are sanctuaries of federal land set aside to preserve habitats.

» Where are these sanctuaries located in the region you are researching?

▸▸ How do federal lands become national wildlife refuges?

▸▸ Do you believe that wildlife refuges will continue to exist as human populations grow and open land becomes more scarce? Explain.

Products

Every group answers these questions.

▸▸ Do any species found in this biome contribute to the making of a product such as medicine, jewelry, clothing, or an everyday or industrial product?

▸▸ Is this use contributing to the endangerment of this species? Explain.

▸▸ Are any species that were found here now extinct because of overuse for manufacture?

▸▸ Describe how these products are of benefit to humans.

Written Reports

There are *two* written reports for *each* student to complete. Use the notes you made from the research you gathered.

▸ **Report One:** Describe the biome your group researched, and illustrate it with pictures of the plant and animal life. Include the following information:

Location, climate, and unique features

How have humans adversely affected the environment of the biome?

Describe how the animals and plants have adapted to conditions.

▸ **Report Two:** Your teacher will give you a name, address, and Internet URL for an organization or government agency involved in wildlife protection. Access the Web site to find the following information and include it in your report:

The kind of work the organization or agency does and the kinds of wildlife they are responsible for in the region you are studying.

What, if anything, is currently being done to protect this habitat?

What can be done to further protect the endangered species in this area?

How would these actions affect the human population in the area?

What are the advantages and disadvantages of these actions?

What laws have been created to protect endangered species?

How have these laws affected the endangered species?

How have they affected people?

What additional laws should be passed?

How can students influence laws?

Send an e-mail message to find additional information or any answers you were unable to find at the Web site.

Compare and Contrast the Biomes

Questions for class discussion follow:

- What is the difference between a biome and an ecosystem?

- In which biome do you live?

- Which biome is the largest in the United States?

- Which is the second largest?

- Which is the smallest?

- Are there any species of plants or animals that are found in more than one biome?

- How does the topography of the biome affect the climate and vegetation found there?

- Which biomes are most at risk? From what?

- What part do humans play in putting these areas at risk?

- What can be done to stop the destruction?

- Are there enough sanctuaries available to protect all the endangered species in the United States? Explain, citing evidence from your research.

- Why is it important to maintain the diversity of the biome?

- How can people's needs be met while conserving wildlife?

▶▶|

ACTIVITY SHEET 8-5
CREATING A DATABASE

Everyone in the class has now completed the assignment, and you are now ready to compare all the biomes that you researched and wrote about by using your computer to create a database. Your teacher and librarian will give you instructions for the database software program available in your school.

Understanding Databases

A database is a collection of related information that is organized to allow you to easily find the information you're looking for. This database will be a comparison of the biomes each group studied, and every student will have the opportunity to input the data he or she found.

Parts of a Database Program

▶ **File**. Another word for database. Your school has a file of all the students in every grade. A database would be able to tell you a student's class, home address, telephone number, and last year's final grades.

▶ **Record**. One unit of related pieces of information. For example, your name, address, class, and last year's final grades would make up one record.

▶ **Field**. A category of information in the record that has a specific characteristic. In the example above, your name is a field, your address is another field, and your class would be the third field.

▶ **Form**. Allows information to be input one field at a time.

▶ **List**. Lets you see many records at one time. Example: All the seventh-grade students in your school.

▶ **Sort**. Arranges the records in any order you want. Example: The principal might want a list of everyone in the seventh grade with an "A" in history.

▶ **Report**. A printout that can be created by combining different data. Example: A printout of all seventh graders living within one mile of the school.

Creating the Database

What kinds of information should be included to make the database useful and easy to use?

▶ List all the categories of information you found during your research.

▶ Brainstorm first with your group and then with the class to decide which of the categories in your journals you want to use as fields.

▶ In a database the most important piece of information is first.

➠ What do you think will be the first field in the database the class is creating?

➠ How many fields do you need?

➠ What name or heading will you use for each field? Some suggestions follow:

   ✓ The name of the biome your group researched.

   ✓ Endangered animals

   ✓ Climate

   ✓ Location

➠ What other field do you want to include?

Using the Database

The database you have just constructed gives you a clear picture of the different biomes that the class researched. You can now compare them to see their differences and similarities.

Use the database to answer the following questions:

➠ In which biome would you most like to live? Why?

➠ In which would you never want to live? Why?

➠ Which biome is most similar to the place where you live?

➠ Which is most different?

➠ In which biome would most of the students in your class like to live?

➠ Rate the biomes that the class most likes and dislikes.

➠ Which regions of the United States are most popular? Why is this?

➠ Which has the most endangered animals and plants?

Evaluating Your Database

➠ Do you have enough fields in the database to be able to answer all the questions?

➠ Should any be added or removed?

➠ Should the headings be changed?

➠ Come up with suggestions for improving the database.

WEB SITES

The Internet is filled with lots of great information about the environment and endangered species. What follows is a selected list of the best online sources.

Department of Interior. ***U.S. Fish & Wildlife Service Home Page***. n.d. Available: www.fws.gov/. (Accessed October 20, 2000). Look here for information on endangered species and much more.

Ecosystems of Our World. n.d. Available: http://library.thinkquest.org/11353/ecosystems.html. (Accessed October 20, 2000). Links to the biomes, information on how humans have affected them, and endangered animals.

EnviroLink. ***Home Page***. © 2000. Available: www.envirolink.org/. (Accessed October 20, 2000). Features "Connect: The Youth Environmental Community"; links to organizations and government agencies.

Environmental Education. ***eelink***. n.d. Available: http://eelink.net/. (Accessed October 20, 2000). Links to sites, searches, classroom resources, and much more for grades K–12.

The National Park Service. ***NatureNet: The National Park's Service's Natural Resource Place On the Net***. Updated October 18, 2000. Available: www.nature.nps.gov/. (Accessed October 20, 2000). Information about wildlife and plants found in the national parks, with links to individual parks.

Sierra Club. ***Home Page***. © 2000. Available: www.sierraclub.org/. (Accessed October 20, 2000). Links to lots of environmental issues, plus the newsletter and magazine.

Sierra Club Books for Children. n.d. Available: www.sierraclub.org/books/. (Accessed October 20, 2000). Link from Sierra Club *Home Page*. Excellent bibliography for readers at all levels.

U.S. Environmental Protection Agency. ***(EPA) Homepage***. Updated October 18, 2000. Available: www.epa.gov/. (Accessed October 20, 2000). *For Kids*—links to *Explorer's Club*, loaded with information about wildlife and the environment. Also links to 10 regions around the United States, and much more.

Chapter Nine

DOES THE PUNISHMENT FIT THE CRIME? THE DEATH PENALTY

By 1967 capital punishment had nearly been abolished in the United States. In 1972 the U.S. Supreme Court ruled that capital punishment laws, as then enforced, were unconstitutional. A later Supreme Court ruling, however, upheld the constitutionality of capital punishment, and many states have since passed laws that meet the court's requirements of specifying the crimes or circumstances for which the death penalty is to be invoked. Thirty-seven states now have laws authorizing the death penalty, as does the military. It is outlawed in most of Europe, Canada, Australia, and most other countries in the world, but because of rising crime rates it is supported by a large number of people in this country.

The fundamental questions raised by the death penalty are whether it is an effective deterrent to violent crime and whether it is more effective than the alternative of long-term imprisonment. People opposed to the death penalty claim that capital punishment constitutes cruel and unusual punishment in violation of the Eighth Amendment and is used unfairly. Women are rarely executed. Those most likely to be sentenced to death are an unfair number of nonwhites, people who are poor or friendless, and those with inexperienced or court-appointed lawyers. In addition, it cannot be proved to better protect the community than does life imprisonment, and errors sometimes lead to the execution of innocent people.

Those persons favoring capital punishment claim that it discourages people from committing crime and that life imprisonment is not an effective deterrent. In addition, life imprisonment puts prison staffs, fellow prisoners, and the community in danger because murderers may escape or be pardoned or paroled.

This chapter examines the pros and cons of the death penalty. Students will use print and online magazines and newspapers to find current information about the issue, take notes, summarize their findings, and finally engage in a debate using the information gathered from the research. They will also find information about the laws in the state in which they live, and e-mail elected officials on all levels to find out where they stand on the issue and if their feelings about the subject are based on evidence or ruled by public opinion.

In preparation for the debate, each student will write a report taking either side of the issue while anticipating the opposition's arguments. Students will revise their papers and exchange them with a partner for peer review before writing the final essay.

Debating involves students in research, provides a way for them to work together toward a shared goal, and enhances their oral communication skills.

PROCEDURE

Materials

Articles from newspapers and magazines, pamphlets, Web resources, nonfiction books, print and nonprint encyclopedias, word processing software, notebooks

Equipment

Computer with Internet access

Curriculum Connections

Social studies, language arts, technology

Objectives

Students will:

- ▶ understand the assignment and the information needed to complete it.
- ▶ identify appropriate information resources.

- ▶ develop categories of related information from a variety of resources.
- ▶ evaluate resources for accuracy and reliability.
- ▶ e-mail elected officials for opinions about the issue.
- ▶ compare and contrast information from many resources for reliability and bias.
- ▶ demonstrate an understanding of the issue.
- ▶ differentiate between fact and opinion.
- ▶ organize and summarize notes made from a variety of sources.
- ▶ analyze arguments both pro and con.
- ▶ recognize the difference between evidence and interpretation.
- ▶ apply the completed research to writing a persuasive essay.
- ▶ evaluate an essay written by another student and offer constructive criticism.

Preparation

This chapter is concerned with teaching students to explore conflicting ideas about an issue, evaluating all the facts while learning to distinguish reliable evidence. The debate about the death penalty is an issue that seems to be in the news almost every day. Begin by developing a bulletin board with articles culled from magazines and newspapers, have students watch television news reports about the issue, and discuss it in class, having them express their opinions.

Activities

Activity One

Discuss the assignment with the class; answer and clarify all questions and concerns. Be sure that students understand what the assignment entails before they begin their research. Students should work in groups but maintain individual notebooks divided into categories of arguments and evidence both for and against the death penalty and use a wide variety of resources to find information, both print and online.

Activity Two

The research process begins here. It's very important for this assignment that all the arguments and evidence be organized in separate categories to enable easy access to the notes when students begin summarizing their findings. Where the information came from is also very important, as this is an issue filled with emotion, and students should understand that not everything they read is factual. Many organizations involved in this issue have Web sites. A list is found at the end of the chapter. More complete instructions for Web evaluation are found in **Chapter One**, "Propaganda."

Activity Three

After each student is certain that he or she has all the necessary information, he or she should begin writing the persuasive essay that tells why he or she believes as he or she does about the death penalty. In addition to expressing an opinion and stating evidence for that opinion, the student must be able to anticipate any arguments that may be presented by the opposition in preparation for the debate. At some time during the writing process, confer with each student to make sure that all points have been covered, that quotes from authorities are included, and that the bibliography is complete. Instructions for peer review are included in this activity sheet.

Activity Four

Discuss the structure and rules of the debate in class so that everyone will be familiar with the procedure. This activity sheet presents a model that you may want to modify, depending on the class's ability. At this age the focus of the debate should not be on the competition but on developing oral communication and reasoning and critical thinking skills and encouraging attitudes of tolerance for the viewpoints of others.

All students who are not selected as debaters will act as judges. Emphasize that the winning side is not necessarily the side with which the judges agree, but rather the side that did the best debating. Judging the debate should be on the basis of evidence and content and must be not only a comparison of the two positions but a conflict that contrasts two opposing views. Students must not just give speeches, they must be ready to respond to evidence presented by the opposition. It's important that when students do their research they anticipate what the other side's arguments will be, so that they are ready to step in with rebuttals. When the class evaluates the debate, in addition to the class discussion students should each be responsible for a written evaluation. You might want students to practice using a tape recorder. Speeches should not be memorized, although using a few index cards to jot down notes is okay. Be sure to videotape the debate for parents and workshops.

ASSESSMENT CHECKLIST

Student's Name _____ Class _____ Date _____

Activity Sheet 9-1   Date Checked _____

➠ Did the student:

✓ fully understand the assignment? YES __ NO __

✓ develop appropriate research questions? YES __ NO __

✓ begin to find print resources? YES __ NO __

✓ have a notebook prepared and divided into categories for each argument? YES __ NO __

✓ understand the criteria that will be used for the final grade? YES __ NO __

➠ The student is permitted to go on to Activity 9-2. YES __ NO __

➠ If the student is not permitted to continue, note the areas of concern and further work that needs to be done.

_____

_____

_____

Activity Sheet 9-2   Date Checked _____

➠ Did the student:

✓ have a list of keywords to use for beginning research? YES __ NO __

✓ understand the necessity of evaluating all sources? YES __ NO __

✓ understand how to distinguish facts from opinions? YES __ NO __

✓ bookmark all the Web sites he or she wants to save? YES __ NO __

✓ follow instructions for taking notes from a Web page? YES __ NO __

✓ include a summary of all the notes for each category? YES __ NO __

✓ use a sufficient number of resources? YES __ NO __

✓ quote from authorities used in the summaries? YES __ NO __

✓ complete the bibliography? YES __ NO __

✓ include a comparison of the resources that reflects an understanding of the issue? YES __ NO __

✓ send an e-mail message to a lawmaker and include the information from that message in his or her notes? YES __ NO __

➠ The student is permitted to go on to Activity 9-3. YES __ NO __

➼ If the student is not permitted to continue, note the areas of concern and further work that needs to be done.

_____

_____

_____

Activity Sheet 9-3   Date Checked _____

➼ Did the student:

    ✓ include valid arguments for the side of the issue taken in his or her essay? YES __ NO __

    ✓ anticipate arguments that the other side might use? YES __ NO __

    ✓ include quotes from authorities? YES __ NO __

    ✓ revise the essay following instructions outlined on the activity sheet? YES __ NO __

    ✓ contribute meaningful suggestions for his or her partner's essay? YES __ NO __

    ✓ change the essay in accordance with any valid suggestions that were made by his or her partner? YES __ NO __

    ✓ write a complete summary of the reviewed essay that included the specific things that needed correction, an explanation of what is missing or unclear, and suggestions for improvement? YES __ NO __

➼ The student is permitted to go on to Activity 9-4. YES __ NO __

➼ If the student is not permitted to continue, note the areas of concern and further work that needs to be done.

_____

_____

_____

Activity Sheet 9-4   Date Checked _____

➼ Did the student:

    ✓ contribute to the class discussion of the rules and structure to be used for the debate? YES __ NO __

    ✓ fulfill his or her role, if a debater for the affirmative side? YES __ NO __

    ✓ anticipate, as a negative debater, the arguments that the affirmative side would present? YES __ NO __

    ✓ fulfill the role, if a rebuttalist? YES __ NO __

    ✓ listen carefully and completely and judge properly and fairly, if a judge? YES __ NO __

    ✓ write an evaluation of the debate? YES __ NO __

    ✓ contribute meaningfully to the class discussion after the debate? YES __ NO __

Final Assessment   Date _____

➤ Did the student:

  ✓ contribute meaningful suggestions to class and group discussions? YES __ NO __

  ✓ use appropriate sources? YES __ NO __

  ✓ complete all the activity sheets and staple them neatly into the notebook, with the answers to all the questions? YES __ NO __

  ✓ answer all the questions on the activity sheets? YES __ NO __

  ✓ have both the essay and the revision in the notebook? YES __ NO __

  ✓ bookmark all the Web sites accessed? YES __ NO __

  ✓ fulfill the debate assignment? YES __ NO __

  ✓ complete all the following written reports, indicating an understanding of the issue researched? YES __ NO __

   • Activity 9-2: A summary of the notes in each category written in complete sentences; a comparison of the resources.

   • Activity 9-3: The first copy of the essay and the revision; a summary of the peer review.

   • Activity 9-4: A written evaluation of the debate.

FINAL GRADE _____

  NOTES _____

  _____

ACTIVITY SHEET 9-1
PLANNING YOUR RESEARCH

Your class has been discussing the death penalty, and you know that this is a subject about which people feel very deeply and hold very strong opinions. But are those opinions based on facts or on feelings?

Vocabulary

- argument
- emotion
- evidence
- persuasive
- clarify
- essay
- peer

Understanding the Assignment

Working in groups, each student will research the issue of the death penalty, finding arguments and evidence both pro and con.

After the research is complete, each student will write a persuasive essay based on the research, taking one side of the dispute. After your first revision you will exchange your essay with a classmate for peer review.

Selected students will participate in a debate about the issue. All students who do not take part in the debate will be judges and participate in a class discussion to evaluate the debate.

All the information should be kept in a separate notebook, with a bibliography of all the resources you used to gather your information. Each argument and all evidence should be kept in a separate category. All activity sheets should be stapled in the notebook, along with completed answers to all questions.

What Information do You Need?

Discuss the assignment with your group, making sure that you understand it. If you have any questions, be sure to ask your teacher to clarify the assignment.

Brainstorm and discuss with your group what you already know about the topic, listing everything that comes to mind. You can always get rid of what you don't need later, so be sure to list everything, no matter how inappropriate it may seem at the time.

Prepare a list of questions that need to be answered. Some questions to think about follow:

- What are the arguments that each side gives for its position?

- What evidence does each side provide to back up its arguments?

- What organizations are involved in the debate?

➼ Who are the authorities on both sides of the issue?

➼ How do lawmakers in your community, state, and federal governments feel about this issue?

➼ Are there any facts that each side agrees with? What are they?

➼ How do the sides disagree on their understanding of the facts?

➼ On what do they base these differences?

As you do your research, keep writing down all the ideas and questions that you think of and enter them in your notebook, *placing each argument in a separate category.*

Where Will You Find the Information?

▶ **Encyclopedias**. Print, online, or CD-ROM encyclopedias for background information.

▶ **Almanacs**. Statistics.

▶ **Newspaper and magazine articles**. Because this is a topic that is in the news so frequently, be sure to read the newspapers daily to see if you can find any information.

▶ **Internet**. Many magazines and newspapers have passages from their current and past issues online. Some magazines give additional information online about various issues that didn't appear in the print edition. Organizations involved in the issue often have Web sites. Your teacher will give you a list of Web sites to use. Federal lawmakers can be reached through e-mail. Some state and local officials also maintain e-mail addresses. If you can't find one that can be reached by e-mail, make contact by telephone or letter.

▶ **School library**. Databases such as SIRS or Ebsco may be available in your school library.

▶ **Additional resources**. Nonfiction books and videos are available in your school and public libraries.

How Your Final Grade Will Be Determined

▶ Participation in all class and group discussion.

▶ A bibliography that indicates the use of appropriate sources.

▶ All activity sheets being stapled neatly into the notebook, with the complete answers to all the questions.

▶ Fulfillment of your assigned role during the debate.

▶ Required written reports:

Activity 9-2: A summary of the notes in each category written in complete sentences; a comparison of the resources.

Activity 9-3: A final essay that includes arguments and evidence for the side you are taking on the issue, anticipates what the other side's arguments will be, and includes quotations from authorities on the subject; a summary of the peer review you gave to your classmate.

Activity 9-4: A written evaluation of the debate.

ACTIVITY SHEET 9-2
DOING THE RESEARCH

You're looking for information not only to better understand the issue of the death penalty but also to find arguments that provide evidence for both sides of the issue. When your research is complete, based on the evidence you found, you'll decide which side of the issue you'll take in your final essay.

Vocabulary

→ anticipate   → factual

→ bibliographic   → format

→ essay

Before You Begin Your Research

Review with your group all the ideas that you want to include in your essay and put all the related ideas into one category. Each category should be in a separate part of your notebook on a separate page. As you do your research, keep adding to the categories and begin new ones as needed. As you find the information, be sure to list all bibliographic information, such as the author, title, date, and page number of articles and all URLs. Check with your teacher to see what format he or she wants you to use for your bibliography. Remember, if you don't use the information from a source for your final report you can always discard it later, but it's next to impossible to go back and find a source you forgot to list.

Make a list of all the keywords you'll use as you look for information.

Evaluating Sources

Not all the sources you use for your research are equal. Some are more factual than others. Many will provide opinions and biases that don't offer accurate evidence for the argument they present. To recognize accurate information you must know if the person or organization responsible for the Web page or the author of an article is an authority on the subject or has gotten the information from a reliable source, and if the information is up-to-date.

It's important to use more than one source of information and get more than one point of view, and also to identify points of agreement and disagreement among sources.

When you write your paper you will not only present the evidence for your argument, you must also be able to anticipate what the other side is going to argue.

Ask yourself:

→ How do I know that the source of this information is reliable?

➠ Is this evidence relevant?

➠ Is relevant evidence left out?

Using the Internet

Your teacher or librarian will give you URLs for the Web sites to search. You may also be permitted to use search engines to find additional information. E-mail elected officials on all levels to find out where they stand on the issue.

Before you start your research, be sure that you understand how to bookmark the sites you search. It's a good idea to make a new folder for your bookmarks and save them as you search. Then delete any bookmarks that you didn't use.

Taking Notes from a Web Page

Printing from the Browser

If you want to take notes offline, print out the entire Web page and any useful links. Remember to make sure that your computer is set to print out the page title, URL, and date.

"Saving as" a File

If the printer isn't available when you need it, you may want to save the Web page on a floppy disk or the hard drive and make notes offline. If you do this, be sure to copy the page title, date you accessed it, and the Web address.

Copying and Pasting to a Word Processor

To make notes while online you can use word processing software while you use your browser. When you find information you want to save, drag the mouse over it and copy it, then use your word processing program to paste it. Be sure to also copy and paste the Web address, title, and the date, so you can return to it if you need to.

Taking Notes

You'll take notes from all your sources and then summarize the notes you made from each article that you use. Arrange all the new information in categories with the information you already have. You'll need quotes to use during the debate if you are selected to be a debater, but use them sparingly and only from reliable sources.

Remember, some articles will just repeat information that you already have, and some will not help you at all. You don't need to write in complete sentences as you take your notes, but include everything you think is important. If you're not sure, include it anyway. You can always discard it later. Keep all your information in categories in your notebook.

For every print magazine, newspaper article, and Web page on which you find information, do the following:

- ▸ Read the entire item very carefully.

- ▸ Write down the title, author, and date of the item.

- ▸ For a Web page, include the site's URL and name.

- ▸ Scan the article or Web page looking for the keywords.

For every reference book you use do the following:

- ▸ Write down the title, author, publisher, and copyright date of the book.

- ▸ Use your list of keywords to help you find your information.

- ▸ Read the table of contents and find the chapters with keywords for your research.

- ▸ Turn to the chapter and scan it.

- ▸ Follow the same directions you used for the articles and Web pages.

Looking for Main Ideas

- ▸ Read the first and last paragraphs. These paragraphs will often have summaries of the main ideas.

- ▸ Read any headings. These will tell you the main points the author is making. Are there any words in *italics*? Sometimes authors use italics when they are trying to emphasize an idea.

- ▸ Look for numbered lists. Authors sometimes use numbered lists to help you understand the main points.

- ▸ List any words that are repeated several times. These are often clues to the main idea. Are any ideas repeated using different words?

- ▸ List the words that tell the main idea.

Summarizing

You now have notes from many sources entered in the proper categories in your notebook.

When you summarize the notes you made during your research, put the main ideas that the author wants you to understand in your own words. If you have a problem putting the information in your own words, underline the key or most important words, then put them into your own words. Be sure to include quotes and bibliographic information.

Write a summary for each category of notes you gathered. Be sure to include the author, title, and date of the article you are summarizing. If this is a Web page or link, include the URL. Use complete sentences to describe the author's opinion. Be sure to use quotation marks when you quote anything.

Comparing Your Sources

➠ Which sources were easier to use?

➠ Which was the most reliable?

➠ Which provided the best information?

▸▸▮ ▬▬▬▬▬▬▬▬▬▬▬▬▬

ACTIVITY SHEET 9-3
WRITING THE REPORT

You have now completed your research, read arguments for and against the death penalty, and evaluated the evidence. You have lots of summaries, both pro and con, of the issue that you made from all your notes. You've put all your information into categories and it's now time for you to decide which side presented the better evidence.

Vocabulary

▸ anticipate   ▸ appropriate

▸ credible   ▸ expand

▸ format   ▸ persuasive

▸ refute   ▸ repetitious

Writing the Essay

Review your categories and your summaries. Before you begin to write, ask yourself:

▸ Do I have enough information to begin writing my report?

▸ Are there any categories that don't have enough information or don't have enough evidence to support them?

▸ Did I use information from dependable sources?

▸ Did I include all the bibliographic information in the format that my teacher wants the class to use?

▸ Do I have enough evidence to persuade my readers that mine is the correct view of the issue?

▸ Do I have enough evidence to refute the arguments that will be made by the opposing side?

▸ Is there anything that seems repetitious and can be throw away?

▸ Do I have to go back and find additional sources?

Remember, if your information seemed good at the time you found it but doesn't support your argument, don't use it.

When you begin to write:

» Take the side that you feel is most persuasive, has the most convincing arguments, and presents the most credible evidence.

» Be sure to include an opening sentence that clearly explains the position you will be arguing, either for or against the death penalty.

» Present arguments and evidence for the stand you are taking.

» Anticipate what the opposition will present during the debate and find arguments that refute their evidence.

» Include quotes from authorities that can be used during the debate.

» Don't put quotes in your own words, but copy them exactly, including the name of the person being quoted.

Revision

Revision doesn't mean only correcting punctuation and grammar; more important, it includes making sure that you got your information across in an interesting way. Read the following list of questions to help you understand which parts of your essay may need to be revised.

» Docs your opening sentence clearly give your position?

» Are all your ideas expressed clearly enough to be understood by someone who is reading about this issue for the first time?

» Are there any arguments that you need to expand with greater detail or with more evidence?

» Is there anything that doesn't seem important to your argument?

» Do you repeat the same arguments in more than one paragraph?

» Should anything be eliminated?

» Did you use one main idea for each paragraph?

» Did you include a topic sentence to introduce the main idea for each paragraph?

» Did you anticipate the arguments that will be used by the opposition and find evidence to challenge their stand?

» Did you use some quotations from reliable sources to support your arguments?

» Does your conclusion let the reader know exactly where you stand on the issue?

» Did you complete your bibliography according to your teacher's instructions?

Revise and rewrite your report now.

Peer Review

You're going to exchange papers with a classmate, read that person's paper, and make constructive suggestions to improve it. Everyone in the class did research into the topic of the death penalty, so when you review your classmate's report you'll have knowledge of the subject and will be able to point out ways that the paper can be improved.

Read the paper through carefully once, looking for positive things to say, before you offer any criticisms. Then go back and mark places that you think are not clear. Suggest ways to correct any problems you find, but don't rewrite the paper. Things to look for include the following:

- ‣ Does the introduction clearly tell how the writer feels about the issue?

- ‣ Are all the ideas clearly expressed?

- ‣ Should any ideas be expanded with greater detail or with more evidence?

- ‣ Should anything be eliminated?

- ‣ Is there a topic sentence used to introduce the main idea for each paragraph?

- ‣ Are the same arguments repeated in more than one paragraph?

- ‣ Is only one main idea used in each paragraph?

- ‣ Did the writer anticipate the arguments and evidence that the opposition may use?

- ‣ Are there quotations from reliable sources?

- ‣ Are the authors of the quotes cited properly?

- ‣ Is the main point made clear and written in an interesting way?

- ‣ Does the writer include information that doesn't have anything to do with the topic or the arguments he or she is making?

- ‣ Does the paper present convincing arguments and evidence?

- ‣ Does the conclusion leave the reader knowing exactly where the writer stands on the issue?

- ‣ Was the assignment completed?

- ‣ How can the report be improved?

- ‣ Check for grammar, punctuation, and spelling mistakes.

- ‣ Did the writer use complete sentences?

- ‣ Is the bibliography complete and correct?

Write a summary of the specific things you believe should be corrected and explain why they need to be corrected. Explain what you don't understand, what you think is missing, what needs to be explained more fully, and what can be cut out.

Don't take it personally if your classmate won't take your suggestions. It's that person's paper, and all you can do is try the best you can to help.

ACTIVITY SHEET 9-4
THE DEBATE

Resolved: The Death Penalty Should Be Abolished.

All the research into the issue and your essay are complete. Your teacher has selected the students who will take part in the debate. Because the entire class did the research and found evidence both supporting and opposing the issue, everyone who is not a debater will act as a judge. Remember, the debate must be a conflict of ideas, and it's important for the debaters to be prepared to refute the other side, not just present their own.

Vocabulary

- affirmative
- rebuttal
- arguments

- extend
- evidence
- rcputable

Structure of the Debate

Each team has three speakers and a rebuttalist. The affirmative side usually begins the debate with a short introduction and with evidence from reputable authorities. Two speakers can divide this task. The third speaker continues the arguments and extends the evidence for the argument. The first speaker then concludes the argument.

The two first negative speakers do pretty much what the affirmatives did, but these students have a tougher job because they can't just give a prewritten speech. They must adapt their arguments to those presented by the affirmative side, telling what the conflict is between the two sides, and begin to refute the affirmative arguments with appropriate evidence. The third negative speaker provides additional evidence for his or her side.

Each side will include a rebuttalist. This is the team's last chance to extend an argument, but new ones can't be presented. The rebuttalist summarizes and tells why his or her side has the better evidence.

Rules

Brainstorm with the class and decide on the rules of the debate. A timekeeper appointed by the teacher will keep track of time, making sure that each speaker doesn't go over the time decided by the class and teacher. Some questions to decide about rules follow:

- Will note passing be permitted among members of the team?

- How much time will be allotted for each speaker?

Judging the Debate

If you are a judge during this debate, listen carefully to both sides. Put aside your own opinion of the issue and concentrate on which side is making the stronger argument and presenting the better evidence. Look for strengths and weaknesses in the arguments given. Winners should be judged on which team had better arguments. Don't let your own opinion get in the way of judgment!

Criteria for Judging

» Were the rules set up by the class adhered to?

» Which side presented the arguments most clearly and had the best evidence?

» Did the opposing team challenge and rebut the other team's arguments?

» Were errors pointed out by the other team?

» Did a team fail to rebut where it could have?

» Was each team's summary convincing?

» Did students speak clearly, convincingly, and slowly enough to be understood?

» Was evidence presented in a way that held the audience's interest?

» If you knew nothing about the topic, could you have understood both pro and con arguments?

Scoring the Debate

Score each category from 1 to 5, with 5 the highest and 1 the lowest.

Affirmative Team

» Did the introduction clearly explain the affirmative side's position? _____

» Was evidence cited to support arguments? _____

» Did the speakers speak clearly and grammatically? _____

» Were the affirmative arguments extended? _____

» Was the affirmative case completed? _____

» Was the negative position refuted? _____

» Rate the overall presentation: _____

» TOTAL_____

Negative Team

⇥ Did the first two speakers adapt their arguments to those presented by the affirmative side? _____

⇥ Was evidence cited for not supporting the affirmative arguments? _____

⇥ Did the speakers speak clearly and grammatically? _____

⇥ Were the negative arguments extended? _____

⇥ Was the negative case completed? _____

⇥ Was the affirmative position refuted? _____

⇥ Rate the overall presentation: _____

⇥ TOTAL _____

Negative Rebuttal

⇥ Was the negative case reviewed? _____

⇥ Were reasons given for the negative case to succeed? _____

⇥ Were reasons given for the affirmative case to fail? _____

⇥ Was the summary convincing and effective? _____

⇥ Rate the overall presentation: _____

⇥ TOTAL _____

Affirmative Rebuttal

⇥ Was the affirmative case reviewed? _____

⇥ Were reasons given for the affirmative case to succeed? _____

⇥ Were reasons given for the negative case to fail? _____

⇥ Was the summary convincing and effective? _____

⇥ Rate the overall presentation: _____

⇥ TOTAL _____

NAME OF JUDGE _____

Class Discussion

Write an evaluation of the debate using the following points, which will be used during class discussion:

» What is your opinion of the death penalty?

» Did the debate make you change your mind about the issue?

» Were any important arguments and evidence not presented? If so, what were they?

» Do you think the scoring was fair?

» Do you agree with the class's judgment? Why?

» How could the arguments have been made stronger?

WEB SITES

Finding information on the Web from organizations opposed to the death penalty is much easier than finding anything from organizations in favor of retaining it.

ACLU [American Civil Liberties Union]. *Death Penalty.* © 1999. Available: www.aclu.org /death-penalty/. (Accessed October 21, 2000).
The ACLU Web site provides articles and data in opposition to the death penalty.

CourtTV. *LegalDocuments: The Death Penalty.* © 2000. Available: www.courttv.com /national/death_penalty/index.html. (Accessed October 21, 2000).
Includes a history of the death penalty and state-by-state information. Related Web sites and news articles.

Death Penalty Information Center. © 1997. Available: www.deathpenaltyinfo.org. (Accessed October 21, 2000).
Huge site with links to women, race, history, and much more.

DeathPenalty.Net. Updated June 4, 1999. Available: www.deathpenalty.net/. (Accessed October 21, 2000).
Lots of links to various subjects related to the death penalty, including a bibliography.

Legal Information Institute at Cornell University. *LII Law About the Death Penalty.* Revised Summer 1998. Available: www.law .cornell.edu/topics /death_penalty.html. (Accessed October 21, 2000).
With links to the "Eighth Amendment: Cruel and Unusual Punishment," U.S. Supreme Court, and other death penalty sites.

▶▶ *Index*

▶▶❘ *About the Author*

Norma Heller is a former school librarian who worked for more than twenty years in one of the first schools in New York City to add computers to the library media center. During that time her students were granted many awards for their creative use of electronic media.

This book is based on *Projects for New Technologies in Education: Grades 6–9* (Libraries Unlimited, 1994). She is also the author of *Technology Connections for Grades 3–5* (Libraries Unlimited, 1998).

Heller received her M. L. S. from Pratt Institute School of Information and Library Science in Brooklyn, New York.